栗 原 は る み

Harumi's Japanese Kitchen

Harumi Kurihara

は じ め に

Foreword

English has never been my strong point and I did not think I would ever study English during my lifetime. However, despite my poor English, in April 2007 I appeared on 'Your Japanese Kitchen', an NHK TV programme broadcast overseas, where I introduced Japanese home cooking. Since then, I have continued to study English with the goal of being able to write my own recipes, and one day express myself, in the English language.

I started teaching cooking twice a year at Kapi'olani Community College of the University of Hawaii in 2014. People often say, 'Japanese cooking is difficult and has so many procedures', or 'Japanese cooking is very time-consuming'. I want to change that image and convey the message that Japanese cooking is fun.

Looking back on my experiences, I have found that English and cooking are, in a sense, very similar. I used to memorise the English phrases I liked to use the most and began to use them in conversation. The same thing can be applied to cooking. Begin by making what you like to eat; you will then gradually become interested in cooking. By cooking for your family and friends or entertaining guests from overseas with your homemade dishes, you can enhance your bonds with other people through food.

The recipes in this book include many of those that I introduced to people outside Japan through the programme 'Your Japanese Kitchen', and those that were most popular when I taught in Hawaii. I have carefully handpicked the recipes that I particularly want people outside Japan to learn. I have tried to explain Japanese dishes simply, beginning with the basic steps, so that people who have never tried Japanese food will be able to understand them. I have also tried to choose ingredients that are available overseas. And I hope that these recipes will also appeal to Japanese people.

In addition to Japanese dishes, I have introduced Japanese cooking utensils and shared my thoughts on things I cherish in my daily life. I would love this book to give more people an opportunity to try Japanese home cooking.

Harumi Kurihara, May 2020

この本の使い方

How to use this book

- Cup measurements in this book are 200 ml. 1 tablespoon is 15 ml and a teaspoon is 5 ml. Level measures are used.

- Weight measurements are given in grams.

- Length measurements are given in cm/mm.

- Measurements are abbreviated as follows:
  tablespoon = tbsp, teaspoon = tsp.

- Quantities described as 'Serves 4' or 'Serves 2' should be treated as estimations.

- In this book, soy sauce refers to regular soy sauce; vinegar refers to white wine vinegar; sugar used is caster sugar; flour refers to plain flour.

- Microwave oven times are estimated using a 600 W model.

- Oven temperatures are provided as Centigrade (°C) and Gas Mark. Ovens should always be preheated.

- Drop-lids are used when simmering dishes, but if you don't have one you can make your own: tear off a sheet of aluminium kitchen foil and fold the edges to make a circle slightly smaller than the inside of your saucepan or frying pan. Pierce the foil with several holes, then place it on top of the food during cooking.

CONTENTS

MEAT & FISH 26

2 VEGETABLES 80

3 RICE, NOODLES & MORE 132

4 DESSERTS 208

白いエプロン
White apron

A white apron is a key item of my work clothing. People tend to avoid wearing white because it can be a challenge to keep it looking white and clean. But this is precisely why I think it is better; it is harder to see stains on a dark-coloured apron. With a white apron, you will need to wash it regularly to keep it free from stains, and this will motivate you to use it with extra care.

This apron is embroidered with my name, so every time I wear it I see my name and it reminds me that I need to be responsible for my own work. And, at the same time, it makes me look forward to another day of cooking.

おいしいご飯を炊きましょう
Let's cook some rice

I like Japanese-style cooked rice, which is why I have experimented with so many different ways to cook perfect rice. Japanese people usually use a rice cooker to cook their rice; however, you can easily cook rice in a saucepan.

There are various ways of preparing rice, but I will introduce you to my own method in this book. I hope you will find your own favourite style by trying several different methods, adjusting the amount of water used, and so on.

ご 飯 の 炊 き 方

How to prepare rice

1. Put 2 cupfuls of Japanese short grain rice in a bowl. Fill with cold water and stir the rice gently with your hand. Drain to discard the cloudy water.

2. Rub the grains gently against each other with the heel of your hand. Rinse under cold running water and drain. Continue rubbing and rinsing until the water becomes clear.

3. Drain the rice in a sieve and let it stand for 15 minutes.

4. Put the rice in a saucepan and add the same volume of water to the pan. For a softer texture, add a little more water; for more bite, use a little less water.

5. Cover the pan and turn the heat to high. Bring to the boil and simmer for 10 –12 minutes over a low heat.

6. Turn off the heat and leave to stand for 10 minutes. Remove the lid and stir the rice.

ご飯が炊けたら
おにぎりに
Onigiri (rice balls)

The rice is cooked – now let's make some *onigiri*. These rice balls made of freshly steamed rice taste especially good. My favourite filling is thinly sliced kelp *tsukudani* (boiled down in sweetened soy sauce). There are many different types of fillings to choose from: *umeboshi* (pickled Japanese plum), grilled salmon, cod roe, dried young sardines seasoned with sansho pepper, and so on – these are all readily available from Asian stores or larger supermarkets. Please feel free to make these rice balls with your choice of fillings.

お に ぎ り

Onigiri (rice balls)

[Serves 4]

cooked rice

nori seaweed

salt

[fillings]

umeboshi
(Japanese pickled plum)

kombu *tsukudani*
(kombu kelp simmered in
salty-sweet sauce)

salted salmon (grilled and
flaked)

*See photograph on pages
14–15*

1. Place some rice on to a piece of clingfilm.
   Make a small dent in the middle with your
   thumb and fill with the filling of your choice
   (about 1 tablespoon). Place more rice on top
   and shape into a ball. Remove the clingfilm.

2. Soak your hands in water and sprinkle a little
   salt on your palms. Then put the rice on it and
   shape into a ball.

3. Wrap the rice balls with nori seaweed.

きちんとだしをとりましょう
Prepare dashi the proper way

Dashi is a Japanese soup stock made from kelp and dried bonito flakes, and is a key component of Japanese cuisine. Recently, dashi stock in the form of powder and tea bags is now available outside Japan, which has helped to spread the popularity of *washoku* (traditional Japanese cuisine). Although I welcome this, I urge you to try authentic dashi made the proper way. As long as you take care with the heating and timing, you can make a tasty dashi – it's easier than you might expect.

だ し の と り 方
How to make dashi (soup stock)

---

10 cm square of kombu kelp

1.2 litres water

40 g dried bonito flakes

1. Rinse the kombu lightly and wipe thoroughly with kitchen paper. Put into a saucepan with the water and leave to soak for about 30 minutes.

2. Place over a high heat. Remove the kombu just before the water comes to the boil. When the water is boiling, add the bonito flakes; when the water boils again, turn the heat off.

3. Leave to stand until the flakes sink to the bottom of the pan, then strain through a sieve.

だしでみそ汁
Miso soup with dashi

_____

If you've made dashi, you can now make miso soup.

I like miso soup so much that I have it every day. I often use leftover ingredients in my miso soup; first I check what's in the refrigerator and then I use whatever combinations of ingredients I have.

In this book, I have included a recipe for the most popular version of miso soup in Japan – tofu and wakame miso soup.

豆腐とわかめのみそ汁

Miso soup with tofu and wakame

[Serves 4]

1 pack silken tofu (about
   350g)

30g wakame seaweed
   (salt-preserved)

800ml dashi (see page 19)

4 tbsp miso (see page 78)

1. Cut the tofu into 1cm cubes. Soak the
   wakame in water to rinse off the salt, then cut
   it into bite-sized pieces. Place the wakame
   into a large soup bowl.

2. Bring the dashi to the boil and add the tofu
   cubes. Add the miso and stir to dissolve.

3. Pour the hot miso soup over the bowl
   of wakame.

箸置き
Hashioki (chopstick rest)

———————————————

This tableware is used to place
chopsticks on the table when
they are not being used. It is
handy to have sets of various
sizes. I enjoy using them in many
different ways – sometimes I use
them to serve garnishes such
as lemon slices or pickles and I
often use the larger-sized ones as
coasters for small glasses.

1

MEAT & FISH

豚のしょうが焼き
Ginger pork

This is a simple and easy dish. I have made it many times and experimented with various methods to create the perfect flavour. The important thing to remember is that you need to take the meat out of the refrigerator so it is at room temperature when you start cooking.

豚 の し ょ う が 焼 き

Ginger pork

[Serves 4]

4 tbsp soy sauce

3 tbsp mirin

1 tbsp grated fresh root
   ginger

300g sliced pork
   fillet or loin *

vegetable oil, for frying

potato salad
   (see page 88)

See photograph on page 29

1. Combine the soy sauce, mirin and grated ginger in a bowl. Marinate the pork in the mixture for a few minutes.

2. Heat some vegetable oil in a frying pan over a high heat and briskly sear both sides of the pork slices until brown. You will need to do this in batches; make sure you pour off any pan juices (reserving the juices) and wipe out the frying pan with kitchen paper between batches.

3. Put some potato salad and the ginger pork on a serving plate. Pour the pan juices from step 2 over the pork.

   * If you can't get sliced pork, half-freeze the pork loin, then slice it as thinly as possible. Place each slice between clingfilm and tap with a rolling pin to make it thinner.

肉 じ ゃ が

Nikujaga (beef and potato stew)

[Serves 4]

4–5 (600g) potatoes

2 onions

250g thinly sliced beef

1 tbsp vegetable oil

300ml dashi (see page 19)

5–6 tbsp soy sauce

3 tbsp mirin

4–4½ tbsp sugar

1 tbsp sake

See photograph on page 32

1. Peel and quarter the potatoes and soak in water for 5–6 minutes, then drain and wipe well with kitchen paper. Cut the onions into 4–6 wedges. Cut the beef into bite-sized pieces.

2. Heat the oil in a frying pan over a medium heat. Add the potatoes and stir-fry until their surface turns translucent. Add the onions and continue to stir-fry.

3. Add the dashi, soy sauce, mirin, sugar and sake and bring to a simmer. Skim the surface and cover with a drop-lid (see page 3). Simmer for 10–12 minutes until the potatoes are soft. Add the beef so that the slices are evenly distributed and cook through. Mix well, then turn off the heat and leave to stand.

肉じゃが

Nikujaga (beef and potato stew)

There are some dishes I cook regularly and discover something new every time; I often say, 'I have never noticed this before'. This is one such dish. It may look easy, but in fact it can be difficult to achieve a balanced flavour.

The most important tip is to stir-fry the potatoes until their surface becomes translucent. This makes it easier for the potatoes to absorb the flavour of the stock and seasonings.

なすと牛肉のみそ煮

Aubergine and beef cooked in miso

Aubergine is the most versatile vegetable because it tastes great cooked in any style, whether stewed, grilled or deep-fried.

I have many favourite aubergine dishes and this recipe is one of them. The rich miso taste goes very well with white rice. By chopping the aubergine into larger bite-sized pieces, you can enjoy the texture of the deep-fried aubergine as it melts in your mouth.

なすと牛肉のみそ煮

Aubergine and beef cooked in miso

[Serves 4]

200g beef steak

7–9 (700g) aubergines

vegetable oil, for deep-frying,
　　plus 1 tablespoon

grated fresh root ginger,
　　to garnish

[sauce]

200ml dashi (see page 19)

3 tbsp soy sauce

3 tbsp mirin

3 tbsp sugar

2–3 tbsp miso (see page 78)

2 tsp *To-Ban-Jan* or any chilli
　　bean paste (see page 79)

See photograph on page 35

1. Combine the dashi and the other ingredients
   for the sauce in a bowl.
2. Cut the beef into bite-sized pieces, if needed.
3. Cut the stems off the aubergines, cut into
   large pieces and soak in water to remove the
   bitterness. Drain well and pat dry. Heat the
   vegetable oil in a deep-sided frying pan and
   deep-fry the aubergines until they are cooked
   through. Remove the aubergine using a slotted
   spoon and drain on kitchen paper.
4. Heat the tablespoon of oil in a separate frying
   pan and sauté the beef.
5. When the beef is cooked, add the sauce.
   When it comes to the boil, add the aubergines.
   Skim the surface, then reduce the heat and
   simmer for 5–10 minutes. Turn off the heat
   and leave to stand for a few minutes.
6. Transfer to a serving bowl, along with the
   sauce, and garnish with some grated ginger.

サーロインステーキのみそづけ
Steak marinated in miso

[Serves 4]

4 sirloin steaks (2 cm thick)

stir-fried vegetables, wasabi
  and sudachi or lime wedges,
  to serve

[miso marinade]

400g miso (see page 78)

100ml sake

200ml mirin

60–80g sugar

See photograph on page 39

1. Make the miso marinade: combine the miso, sake, mirin and sugar in a saucepan and bring to the boil. Keep stirring over a low heat to avoid burning, and reduce down for about 20 minutes until the sauce thickens.

2. Spread 2 tablespoons of the marinade on both sides of each steak and cover with clingfilm. Marinate in the refrigerator for 1–2 days.

3. Scrape the marinade from the steaks with a spatula, then cut the steaks into strips.

4. Grill the steaks on both sides. Serve with stir-fried vegetables, wasabi and sudachi or lime wedges.

   * Leftover marinade can be stored in the refrigerator for up to 3 weeks.

サーロインステーキ
のみそづけ

Steak marinated in miso

Marinating ingredients with miso, a technique called *misozuke* in Japan, is a traditional way of cooking that we have practised in Japan for many years. It is useful as it not only gives richness to the taste but also preserves the food for longer. You can also use fish or vegetables instead of meat.

To avoid burning the meat, cut it into slices about 2 cm wide. This way, you can remove each piece from the heat just in time when it is well cooked.If you like, serve with grated wasabi or *shichimi togarashi* (Japanese seven-spice).

筑 前 煮
Chicken with vegetables
Chikuzen-style

This is a popular dish often served
at New Year; however, in my home
I cook this at any time of the year.
The important point to remember
when cooking this dish is to cut the
ingredients into evenly sized pieces
or slices, and to put them into the
pan in the correct order so that they
cook evenly.

I also wanted to introduce you to
various Japanese ways of cutting
vegetables so I have used several
techniques (see page 228).

筑 前 煮

Chicken with vegetables *Chikuzen*-style

[Serves 4]

4 dried shiitake mushrooms

250g boneless chicken thighs

2 small parsnips or 1 burdock
   root (about 180g)

1 carrot (200g)

1 small bamboo shoot
   (150g), boiled

1 lotus root (200g)

1 block of konnyaku (200g),
   optional

1–2 tbsp vegetable oil

300ml dashi (see page 19)

4 tbsp soy sauce

4 tbsp sugar

2 tbsp mirin

2 tbsp sake

See photograph on page 41

1. Soak the dried shiitake mushrooms in just
   enough hot water to cover them and set aside
   to soften. Squeeze lightly to remove the water.
   Cut off the stems, then cut each one into
   4 pieces.

2. Cut the chicken into bite-sized pieces.

3. Peel the parsnips or burdock root and cut
   diagonally into 2cm pieces. Soak in water
   while you prepare the rest of the ingredients,
   then drain well.

4. Peel the carrot and cut into 2cm half-moons
   (*hangetsu-giri*, see pages 228–230).
   Cut the bamboo shoot into random shapes
   (*ran-giri*, see pages 229–231).

5. Peel the lotus root and cut into 2cm quarter-
   rounds (*icho-giri*, see pages 228–230).
   Soak in water and drain well.

6. Blanch the konnyaku, if using, and drain well.
   Tear into bite-sized pieces when cool.

7. Heat the oil in a deep frying pan and stir-
   fry the chicken. Add, in this order, the
   parsnips, carrot, konnyaku (if using), shiitake
   mushrooms, bamboo shoot and lotus root and
   stir-fry, adding a little more oil if necessary
   between additions.

8. Add the dashi, soy sauce, sugar, mirin and
   sake. Bring to the boil, skim the surface, then
   cover with a drop-lid (see page 3). Simmer
   for about 15 minutes, or until the sauce is
   reduced.

マカロニグラタン
Macaroni gratin

[Serves 4]

250g raw prawns

1 boneless chicken thigh

100g tin mushrooms

100g macaroni

vegetable oil, for frying

½ onion, thinly sliced

150g grated Cheddar cheese

[white sauce]

40g butter

50g flour

500ml milk

200ml double cream

salt and pepper, to taste

vegetable oil, salt,
  and pepper

See photograph on page 44

1. Preheat the oven to 230°C, Gas Mark 8.

2. Remove the shells and devein the prawns. Wash them well and dry thoroughly with kitchen paper.

3. Cut the chicken into bite-sized pieces and drain the mushrooms.

4. Make the white sauce: melt the butter in a large saucepan, add the flour and stir for 2–3 minutes, ensuring it doesn't burn. Gradually pour in the milk and stir constantly for about 5 minutes until it thickens. Add the double cream and cook for a short time. Season with salt and pepper and set aside.

5. Cook the macaroni in boiling water according to the instructions on the pack. When it's done, drain in a colander.

6. Heat a little oil in a frying pan and stir-fry the prawns. Season with a little salt and pepper, then tip them into a dish. Add a little more oil if necessary and stir-fry the chicken, onion and mushrooms in this order, seasoning with salt and pepper.

7. Add the chicken, onion, mushrooms, prawns, and macaroni to the white sauce and mix together.

8. Tip into an ovenproof dish and sprinkle the cheese over the top. Bake in the oven for 15–20 minutes.

マカロニグラタン
Macaroni gratin

This is a common recipe that many Japanese families like to make at home. The Japanese version contains macaroni, prawns, onion, mushrooms and chicken and, in my opinion, is one of the best dishes the Japanese have created.

Topping it with plenty of cheese only makes this even more delicious. I sometimes put a little soy sauce on top, too.

揚 げ 鶏 の ね ぎ ソ ー ス
Fried chicken with leek sauce

This dish has a lot of memories for me as I used to make this for my father who was not usually fond of chicken. This is one of my most popular recipes. The secret to making crispy fried chicken is to take the chicken out of the refrigerator and bring it to room temperature before cooking, and to coat the chicken with plenty of potato starch just before frying. Fry the chicken twice to ensure the centre of the chicken is fully cooked.

揚 げ 鶏 の ね ぎ ソ ー ス
Fried chicken with leek sauce

[Serves 4]

2 boneless chicken thighs,
　skin on

½ tbsp soy sauce

½ tbsp sake

potato starch, for coating
　(see page 79)

vegetable oil, for deep-frying

[leek sauce]

100 ml soy sauce

1 tbsp sake

2 tbsp vinegar

1½ tbsp sugar

1 baby leek or 1 Japanese leek
　or 2 small spring onions

½ tbsp vegetable oil

1 red chilli, chopped

See photograph on page 47

1. Bring the chicken up to room temperature before cooking. Pierce the chicken skin in several places with a fork, then cut each thigh in half. Put into a dish with the soy sauce and sake and leave to marinate.

2. Make the sauce: mix the soy sauce, sake, vinegar and sugar together in a bowl. Chop the leek or spring onion finely. Heat the oil in a frying pan and stir-fry the spring onion and red chilli. Stir constantly, then add the soy sauce mixture and remove from the heat.

3. Heat the oil for deep-frying to 180 °C in a large saucepan. Remove the chicken from the marinade and dredge thoroughly with potato starch. Deep-fry the chicken for 2–3 minutes, then remove and put on a wire rack for about 4 minutes – it will continue to cook with the residual heat. Then deep-fry it again for 1–2 minutes over a high heat.

4. Drain and cut the chicken into bite-sized pieces. Place on a serving plate and pour the sauce over the top.

和風マーボー豆腐

Japanese-style *mabo-dofu*

[Serves 4]

2 packs silken tofu
(about 700g)

1 tbsp potato starch
(see page 79)

1 tbsp water

2 tbsp vegetable oil

1 tbsp grated garlic

1 tbsp grated fresh root ginger

4 tbsp finely chopped baby leek
or Japanese leek or spring
onions

200g mix of minced beef and
minced pork

sesame oil, for drizzling

2–3 red chillies, sliced or
sansho powder, to garnish

[sauce]

300ml dashi (see page 19)

4–5 tbsp soy sauce

2 tbsp mirin

1 tbsp sugar

See photograph on page 51

1. Cut the tofu into 1.5cm cubes. Bring a saucepan of water to the boil, add a little salt and boil the tofu in it for about 2 minutes before draining in a colander.

2. Mix the potato starch and water together until dissolved.

3. Combine the ingredients for the sauce in a saucepan and heat.

4. Heat the vegetable oil in a frying pan and stir-fry the garlic, ginger and leek or spring onions. Once they become fragrant, add the minced beef and pork mixture and stir-fry. When the meat is cooked through, pour the sauce in; when it comes to a boil, add the dissolved potato starch and let it thicken. Add the tofu and mix gently. Drizzle sesame oil over the pan.

5. Serve on a plate, garnished with red chilli slices, or *sansho* powder, if preferred.

和風マーボー豆腐
Japanese-style *mabo-dofu*

I love mabo-dofu. This one uses Japanese-style dashi as a substitute for Chinese soup, giving it a mild flavour.

The mixture can be frozen before the tofu is added, making this convenient to prepare ahead – simply reheat in a pan and add some cooked tofu before serving.

牛肉コロッケ
Beef and potato croquettes

Cooking the onion and beef in butter and adding them to the potatoes along with their juices means the potatoes will be full of flavour. The onion should not be cut too finely, nor should it be cooked for too long – this will ensure that the onion will retain some texture and bite.

As potatoes are the main feature of this dish, try this recipe using floury potatoes such as Desiree, King Edward or Maris Piper.

牛 肉 コ ロ ッ ケ

Beef and potato croquettes

[Makes 20]

4 potatoes (500g)

1 onion (200g)

200g beef trimmings

30g butter

vegetable oil for deep-frying

salt and pepper, to taste

[coating]

flour, beaten eggs,
    panko breadcrumbs

[coleslaw]

200g shredded white cabbage

1 tbsp lemon juice

2 tbsp olive oil

salt and pepper

[to serve]

3 tbsp *tonkatsu* sauce
    (shop-bought)

2 tbsp tomato ketchup

Japanese mustard or English
    mustard

See photograph on page 53

1. Peel and cut each potato into 4–6 pieces. Soak them in water for a few minutes, then drain. Line a microwave-safe bowl with some kitchen paper and add the potatoes. Cover loosely with clingfilm and microwave for 5–6 minutes until tender.

2. Remove the clingfilm and kitchen paper from the bowl. Mash the potatoes while hot.

   * If you want to boil in a saucepan instead of using a microwave, see page 90.

3. Cut the onion into 1cm square pieces. Cut the beef into 2cm square pieces. Heat the butter in a frying pan and stir-fry the beef. Add the onion and continue to stir-fry. Season with ½ teaspoon salt and a little pepper.

4. Add the beef mixture and juices to the mashed potatoes. Season to taste with salt and pepper and mix well.

5. Shape into balls. Coat with flour, beaten egg and then breadcrumbs. Heat the oil for deep-frying in a saucepan to 170°C and deep-fry the croquettes until crispy. Drain on kitchen paper.

6. Mix all the coleslaw ingredients together and put on a plate along with the croquettes.

7. Mix together the tonkatsu sauce and ketchup to make a sauce. Serve the croquettes with the sauce and mustard.

豚カツ

Tonkatsu (breaded pork)

[Serves 4]

½ head white cabbage

1 kg pork shoulder or loin, about 2 cm thick

vegetable oil, for deep-frying

salt and pepper

[coating]

flour, beaten eggs,
   panko breadcrumbs

[to serve]

tonkatsu sauce (shop-bought)

Japanese mustard or English mustard

lemon wedges

See photograph on page 56

1. Finely shred the cabbage and soak in iced water to make it crispy. Drain, put it in a plastic food bag and chill in the refrigerator until ready to serve.

2. Slice the pork into slices about 2 cm wide. Slash the sinew running between the fat and lean tissue with a knife to prevent it from shrinking when deep-fried. Season with salt and pepper.

3. Dust the pork slices with flour, dip them in beaten egg, then coat with breadcrumbs.

4. Heat the oil in a saucepan to 170 °C. Deep-fry the pork until golden brown on the outside and cooked through. Drain on kitchen paper.

5. Cut the fried pork into bite-sized pieces. Serve with the cabbage, *tonkatsu* sauce and Japanese mustard. It's also tasty with a squeeze of lemon and some salt.

豚 カ ツ
Tonkatsu (breaded pork)

Tonkatsu is deep-fried breaded pork. When I cook *tonkatsu*, I always make much more than my family can eat and I keep the rest in the freezer for unexpected visits from friends.

If you prepare various sizes of *tonkatsu*, from bite-sized to larger strips, they can be used for a variety of recipes. I often make *tonkatsu* using one large piece of pork and serve it on a platter to be sliced and shared at the table. But when I make the rice bowl dish *katsu-don*, I make bite-sized *tonkatsu*, because the extra coating absorbs more sauce and makes it tastier.

さばのみそ煮
Mackerel cooked in miso

_____

This is one of the most popular and basic dishes in Japanese home cooking. However, my version is cooked with light miso sauce, which goes well with bread as well as with plain steamed white rice. I sometimes serve this with slices of garlic bread to soak up the delicious sauce.

I like to cut the mackerel into small pieces rather than large ones – that way, I can savour each bite.

さばのみそ煮

Mackerel cooked in miso

[Serves 4]

1 fresh mackerel (400g/ prepared weight)

2.5cm piece of fresh root ginger

100ml sake

100ml water

3 tbsp sugar

1 tbsp soy sauce

4 tbsp mirin

5–6 tbsp miso (see page 78)

See photograph on page 59

1. First, fillet the mackerel into three pieces*: Cut off the head and remove the innards. Wash thoroughly and wipe dry with kitchen paper. Then, keeping the knife flat, cut horizontally from the tail along the side of the spine to remove the top fillet. Turn it over and repeat on the other side. Remove any bones. Cut each fillet diagonally into three equal pieces (see *sogi-giri,* pages 232–234).

   * Filleting a fish into three pieces means two pieces of flesh and one of bone.

2. Peel the ginger and thinly slice.

3. Put the sake and water in a saucepan and place over a medium heat. When the alcohol has boiled off, add the sugar, soy sauce, mirin and miso and stir together. When it comes to the boil, place the mackerel in the pan along with the sliced ginger. When the sauce comes to the boil again, cover with a drop-lid and simmer for 10–15 minutes over a low heat.

4. When the sauce is reduced and becomes syrupy, it is ready. Arrange the mackerel in a bowl and pour the sauce and ginger slices over the top.

銀 だ ら の 香 り 煮

Aromatic black cod

[Serves 4]

4 –5 black cod or salmon fillets
  (450–500g)

1 tbsp grated garlic

1 tbsp grated fresh
  root ginger

½ Japenese leek or 1 spring
  onion, chopped

[seasonings]

4 tbsp soy sauce

2 tbsp sugar

4 tbsp sake

4 tbsp mirin

1 tsp miso (see page 78)

1–2 tsp *To-Ban-Jan* or any
  chilli bean paste (see
  page 79)

[to serve]

shungiku (Japanese greens),
  or spinach or rocket leaves

wakame seaweed

See photograph on page 63

1. First separate the leaves from the stems of the
   shungiku. Soak the leaves in iced water to
   crisp. Drain well.

2. Cut the wakame into bite-sized pieces. Mix
   with the *shungiku*, transfer to a serving plate
   and chill in the refrigerator

3. Pat the black cod or salmon dry with kitchen
   paper, then cut each fillet in half.

4. Combine the seasonings in a wide saucepan
   and bring to the boil. Add the fish, making
   sure to avoid piling the pieces on top of each
   other.

5. When it comes to the boil again, add the
   garlic, ginger and leek or spring onion. Cover
   with a drop-lid (see page 3), reduce the heat
   and simmer for about 10 minutes over a
   low heat.

6. Place the salmon on top of the *shungiku* and
   wakame and pour the piping hot sauce over
   the top.

銀だらの香り煮
Aromatic black cod

People often seem to think that the cooking technique *nizakana* (cooking fish in broth) is a bit more difficult compared to other Japanese dishes. But this is a very easy recipe, so I'd like you to try it. Once you learn the balance of the ingredients for the broth, you can try cooking it with different varieties of fish.

The hot broth poured over raw *shungiku* and wakame turns this into an unexpected delicacy.

さけとえびのつくね
Salmon and prawn balls

Every time I travel to other countries, I am always amazed by how much people love salmon and prawns. This is a recipe I came up with when I was abroad. The mixture can also be shaped and cooked on skewers like *yakitori* or made into patties for burgers.

さけとえびのつくね
Salmon and prawn balls

[Makes 10]

3 salmon fillets (300 g)

10 raw, shelled prawns
(200 g)

½ onion

1 tbsp sake

vegetable oil, for frying

salt and pepper, to taste

[lemon *ponzu* sauce]

5 cm square of kombu kelp

100 ml mirin

100 ml soy sauce

4 tbsp lemon juice

[salty-sweet sauce]

50 ml soy sauce

50 ml mirin

2 tbsp sugar

[to serve]

2 *sudachi* or limes, halved

sansho (Japanese pepper)
powder

See photograph on page 65

1. Remove the skin from the salmon. Chop it coarsely first and then mince it.
2. Wash the prawns and devein them. Chop them coarsely first and then mince them; I like to mince the tails finely and leave the bodies with some texture.
3. Cut the onion into 8 mm squares.
4. Put the salmon and prawns into a bowl, add the sake, onion and salt and pepper to taste and mix.
5. Shape the mixture into 5 cm rounds. Heat a little oil in a frying pan and pan-fry the balls until they are cooked through.
6. Make the lemon *ponzu* sauce: Rinse the kombu lightly with water and wipe dry. Put the mirin in a saucepan and bring to the boil. Turn down the heat and simmer for a couple of minutes. Transfer to a bowl and add the soy sauce, lemon juice and kombu. Keep in the refrigerator.
7. Make the salty-sweet sauce: Combine all the ingredients in a small saucepan and bring to the boil. Turn down the heat to low and let it simmer for about 5 minutes until it thickens a little.
8. Serve the salmon and prawn balls with sudachi, *sansho* powder and both sauces.

さけの南蛮づけ

Deep-fried salmon marinated in *nanbanzu*

[Serves 4]

1 small carrot (100g)

½ celery stick

½ onion

2 cm piece of fresh
  root ginger

4 salmon fillets (400g)

3 tbsp flour

vegetable oil,
  for deep-frying

2 red chillies, chopped

strips of yuzu zest

salt and pepper, to taste

[*nanbanzu* sauce]

200ml dashi (see page 19)

3 tbsp light soy sauce

150ml vinegar

4 tbsp sugar

salt

See photograph on page 68

1. Cut the carrot into julienne strips about 5 cm long.

2. Destring the celery and cut it into julienne strips about 5 cm long.

3. Slice the onion.

4. Cut the ginger into thin strips.

5. Combine all the ingredients for the *nanbanzu* sauce together in a shallow dish.

   * You can add 1 tablespoon citrus juice, such as yuzu, lemon or sudachi, if liked.

6. Cut the salmon into bite-sized pieces. Sprinkle salt and pepper over the salmon, then toss in the flour to coat completely.

7. Heat the vegetable oil in a saucepan to 170–180°C and deep-fry the salmon pieces. Remove from the oil and immediately put them into the *nanbanzu* marinade while they are still hot. Add the carrot, celery, onion, ginger, red chillies and yuzu zest, cover with clingfilm and put in the refrigerator. Let it stand for a while to marinate before serving.

さけの南蛮づけ
Deep-fried salmon
marinated in *nanbanzu*

Nanbanzuke is a dish in which ingredients are deep-fried and then marinated in a vinegar sauce with thinly sliced vegetables. I like eating lots of vegetables so I use plenty of them in this recipe.

I cook this dish throughout the year and use seasonal citrus fruits, such as yuzu in winter and sudachi or lemons in summer, to add fragrance to the dish.

えびカツ
Ebikatsu (breaded prawns)

These small prawns are more satisfying and have a more appealing look, taste and texture when shaped into patties and deep-fried – just be careful not to overcook the prawns. I often serve this dish – sizzing hot – at parties at my home.

えびカツ

Ebikatsu (breaded prawns)

[Makes 8]

6 tbsp flour

1 egg, beaten

1 tbsp water

24 raw king prawns

panko breadcrumbs, to coat

vegetable oil,
   for deep-frying

salt and pepper, to taste

lemon wedges, to serve

[tartare sauce]

200 ml mayonnaise

1–2 tbsp milk

Japanese mustard or English
   mustard, to taste

3 tbsp pickled cucumber,
   finely chopped

2 hard-boiled eggs,
   finely chopped

¼ onion, finely chopped
   (3 tbsp)

salt and pepper, to taste

1. First make the tartare sauce: put the mayonnaise in a bowl and dilute with the milk. Add a little Japanese mustard and mix. Stir in the pickled cucumber, eggs and onion. Season to taste with salt and pepper.

2. Mix the flour, beaten egg and water together until the mixture becomes paste-like.

3. Remove the shells and tails from the prawns and devein them with a toothpick. Cut the prawns in half lengthways. Use 6 pieces per portion to make round, tight, flat patties. Season with salt and pepper.

4. Using a fish slice, scoop up the patties and coat them in the paste made in step 2. Then coat the patties with breadcrumbs.

5. Heat the oil to 180–190 °C and deep-fry the patties until they are cooked through. Drain on kitchen paper.

6. Serve with the tartare sauce and lemon wedges.

ESSAY
3
エッセイ

さくら I Sakura

さくら
Sakura

[Serves 4]

Spring in Japan reminds me of sakura (cherry blossoms), my favourite flower. Sakura are now widely loved by many people all over the world, not only in Japan. When the weather gets warmer and spring feels like it's just around the corner, I eagerly await the news that the cherry blossoms are in bloom. Once the cherry blossoms have fully opened, the petals soon fall to the ground. They last only for about ten days after the buds have bloomed. Gracious and, although very fragile, the blossoms somehow soothe people's minds.

During cherry blossom season, I put some branches of cherry blossoms in the hallway or in the rooms of my home for decoration, or I pick some petals and set them afloat in a cup of Japanese sake or green tea. Sometimes, I pick a tiny twig with flowers from a sakura tree and place it on the table to use as a chopstick rest. I now have many kinds of tableware and tablecloths with cherry blossom motifs on.

Spring is my favourite season of the year. Many seasonal fish and vegetables become available in the market. When I see sweet-smelling herbs or fresh leafy vegetables I just want to start cooking with them. I like to cherish every moment of this rich and generous season of the year.

本書で使われている主な調味料
Basic ingredients used in this book

しょうゆ Soy sauce

The salty sauce is essential for Japanese recipes and has a unique savoury taste. It is widely used as a dipping sauce, for seasoning cooked food and for adding flavour to Japanese-style sauces. There are various kinds of soy sauce, with regular soy sauce (*koikuchi*) offering a darker colour and less salt compared with light soy sauce (*usukuchi*).

うす口しょうゆ Light soy sauce

This soy sauce, which is favoured in the Kansai area, has medium colour and flavour but is saltier than regular soy sauce. Light soy sauce is in fact the saltiest of all soy sauce varieties. It is mostly used for dishes with pale-coloured vegetables or white fish and for seasoning clear soups, because its colour matches the natural flavour and colour of those ingredients.

穀物酢 *Kokumotsu-su* (rice and grain vinegar)

This is the most commonly used vinegar in Japan. It is made from a blend of rice, wheat and corn and the lees left over from sake production. It has a savoury and sour flavour, and is widely used in Western and Chinese dishes as well as Japanese. At 4.2% it has less acidity than wine vinegar.

料理酒 *Ryori-shu* (cooking sake)

Unlike the sake for drinking, cooking sake is a little sour and has a bit of an odd taste, but it helps to remove any unpleasant smells from fish and meat and provides a deeper flavour to dishes. Some products have added salt or sugar. If you don't have cooking sake, you can use ordinary drinking sake.

みりん Mirin

A sweet alcoholic liquid produced from distilled spirits, steamed glutinous rice and malted rice. Mirin adds sweetness and shine to dishes, but has a milder sweetness and flavour than sugar. The alcohol in mirin prevents simmered ingredients from breaking up too much and also removes any unpleasant smells from meat or fish.

みそ Miso

Miso comes in the form of a paste and is a traditional Japanese seasoning produced from fermented soybeans, rice and wheat. There are several hundred regional variations in taste, colour and flavour of miso paste. In this book, I use *komemiso* (rice miso), which has a yellowish colour, unless specified otherwise.

上白糖 *Johakuto* (refined white caster sugar)

This is the sugar most commonly used in Japanese homes. If the recipe says 'sugar', it usually means this sugar. It is unique to Japan and has finer crystals than granulated sugar and contains some moisture, but regular caster sugar will also work. It has no strong flavour and dissolves easily.

ごま油 Sesame oil

This is made from compressed sesame seeds –regular sesame oil is made from toasted sesame seeds and is darker brown in colour with a strong flavour.

鶏ガラスープの素 Granulated Chinese chicken soup stock

This is ready-made seasoning produced from the essence of chicken soup stock and flavoured with vegetable essence. It is mainly used for Chinese recipes such as soups and sautéed dishes.

豆板醤 *To-Ban-Jan*

A Chinese chilli paste mainly used for Sichuan-style recipes. *To-Ban-Jan* is used to add spiciness and a savoury taste to sautéed dishes, simmered dishes and thick, starchy sauces.

とんかつソース Tonkatsu sauce

This Japanese sauce is mainly used for *tonkatsu* (deep-fried breaded pork) and is similar to Worcestershire sauce, although it is sweeter and thicker.

かたくり粉 *Katakuri ko* (potato starch)

Traditionally Japanese *katakuri ko* was made from the katakuri root, and was named after the plant. Today, starch made from potato is available as a substitute for *katakuri ko*. Potato starch is used as a coating before deep-frying and to thicken soups and sauces. When using it as a thickener, dissolve it in water before use to avoid it from becoming lumpy.

2

野菜のおかず

VEGETABLES

にんじんと
ツナのサラダ

Carrot and tuna salad

I came up with this recipe when I once had a lot of carrots left over and wanted to use up the other ingredients I had in my kitchen. I first made this recipe more than 30 years ago, but it is still a popular dish today.

The carrots are not boiled, nor eaten raw but microwaved. The key to this recipe is to finely chop the onion and garlic.

にんじんとツナのサラダ
Carrot and tuna salad

[Serves 4]

250g carrots

2 tbsp finely chopped onion

1 tsp finely chopped garlic

1 tbsp vegetable oil
or olive oil

30g canned tuna

[dressing]

1 tbsp white wine vinegar

1 tbsp wholegrain mustard

1 tbsp lemon juice

salt and pepper, to taste

1. Cut the carrots into 5–6cm-thin strips. Put them in a microwave-safe bowl and mix in the onion, garlic and oil.

2. Cover loosely with clingfilm and microwave at 600W for 1 minute 20 seconds.

3. Remove the bowl from the microwave and take off the clingfilm. Stir lightly and add the drained tuna and the dressing ingredients. Mix together.

4. Chill in the refrigerator to allow the dressing to soak into the vegetables.

トマトのおひたし

Tomato *ohitashi*

[Serves a crowd]

300 ml dashi (see page 19)

2 tbsp mirin

2 tbsp light soy sauce

400 g tomatoes

See photograph on page 86

1. Combine the dashi, mirin and light soy sauce in a shallow container.

2. Remove the stalks from the tomatoes and then make a small score in the skin of each.

3. Put the tomatoes into a bowl of boiling water for about 10 seconds, then put them into a bowl of cold water. Drain and peel off the skins leaving the tomatoes whole.

4. Add the tomatoes to the dashi mixture, cover with clingfilm, then chill in the refrigerator to allow the tomatoes to absorb the flavours.

トマトのおひたし
Tomato *ohitashi*

Ohitashi is often made with leafy vegetables, but I make it with all kinds of ingredients, such as okra, mushrooms and grated yam, among others. This recipe works for any vegetable, so please feel free to be creative with whatever ingredients are in season and that you have to hand.

ポテトサラダ
Potato salad

There are many variations of potato salad, but this recipe is the simplest and is enjoyed in homes across Japan. The ingredients are easily available in most countries, so you can make it any time, anywhere. The key is to slice the cucumbers slightly thicker for a crunchy texture, not to soak the sliced onions in water for too long and to fold in the mayonnaise gently.

ポ テ ト サ ラ ダ

Potato salad

[Serves 4]

4 –5 potatoes (450 g)

1 small cucumber

½ small onion

2 slices ham

5 –6 tbsp mayonnaise

salt and pepper, to taste

See photograph on page 89

1. Peel and cut each potato into 4 –6 pieces. Soak in water and drain. Line a microwave-safe bowl with some kitchen paper and add the potatoes. Cover loosely with clingfilm and microwave for 5 –6 minutes until tender.

2. Remove the clingfilm and kitchen paper from the bowl. Mash the potatoes while they are hot and allow to cool.

   * To boil the potatoes, first thoroughly wash the unpeeled whole potatoes, put them in a saucepan of cold water, cover and place over a high heat. When the water comes to the boil, turn the heat down to low and cook for 20–25 minutes until tender. Peel the skins off, then transfer the potatoes to a bowl and mash while they are still hot.

3. Slice the cucumber. Toss with a little salt in a bowl and let it stand for 5 minutes. When it starts to soften, use kitchen paper to squeeze out the excess moisture.

4. Thinly slice the onion and soak in water for 5 minutes before squeezing out the excess moisture with kitchen paper.

5. Cut the slices of ham in half and then cut into thin strips.

6. Add the cucumber, onion and ham to the mashed potatoes and mix together. Fold in the mayonnaise and season with salt and pepper to taste.

コールスローサラダ

Coleslaw

[Serves a crowd]

4 – 5 leaves cabbage (400g)

50g carrots

salt and pepper, to taste

[dressing]

6 tbsp mayonnaise

3 tbsp vinegar

1 tsp sugar

See photograph on page 93

1. Cut the cabbage into 1 cm squares and put them into a bowl.

2. Peel the carrots and cut into fine dice, then add to the bowl. Mix in 1 ½ teaspoons salt and leave for 10 – 15 minutes. When the cabbage and carrot have released some moisture, squeeze it out thoroughly using muslin or kitchen paper.

3. Combine the ingredients for the dressing in a bowl.

4. Add the dressing to the bowl of cabbage and carrot and mix well. Season to taste with salt and pepper.

コールスローサラダ

Coleslaw

I like coleslaw that is sour and a bit sweet. It doesn't taste as good if it becomes watery, so it is important to thoroughly squeeze the excess water from the shredded cabbage and carrot before mixing in the dressing.

ほうれんそうの
ピーナツあえ
Spinach with peanut sauce

This dish is made with spinach and peanut butter, both of which are readily available in any country, so this is something I often cook when I am overseas. It is a very simple and easy recipe. Be sure not to overcook the spinach and to thoroughly squeeze the excess water out for the best results.

ほうれんそうのピーナツあえ
Spinach with peanut sauce

[Serves 4]

3 tbsp peanut butter

1 tsp sugar

1 tsp soy sauce

2 tsp mirin

200g large-leaved spinach

salt

chopped peanuts, to serve

1. Mix the peanut butter, sugar, soy sauce and mirin in a bowl.
2. Cut the spinach into 5 cm strips, separating the leaves from the stems. Blanch the stems first in boiling salted water, then add the leaves. Drain and immediately plunge into cold water, then drain again. Squeeze out the excess water.
3. Add the spinach to the peanut sauce and mix together. Taste and add a little salt if necessary.
4. Serve the spinach on a plate and sprinkle coarsely chopped peanuts over the top.

かぶとキウイの
カルパッチョ
Turnip and kiwifruit carpaccio

All you have to do here is to slice the ingredients finely and chill them well in the refrigerator. Then all that is left to do is to arrange them on a plate. This simple dish is ready in just 5 minutes; having several easy recipes like this one will come in handy when you have people over. I entertain my friends by arranging the food on the plate in front of them.

かぶとキウイのカルパッチョ
Turnip and kiwifruit carpaccio

[Serves 4]

2–3 baby turnips

1–2 kiwifruits

salt and pepper, to taste

olive oil, for drizzling

See photograph on page 98

1. Cut the stems off the turnips and peel them, then cut into wafer-thin round slices.
2. Peel the kiwifruits and cut them into thin round slices.
3. Arrange a layer of turnip slices on a serving plate and sprinkle with some salt and pepper. Place a layer of kiwifruit slices on top of the turnip, then add a few more turnip slices on top of the kiwifruit, slightly overlapping them. Chill in the refrigerator until ready to serve.
4. Drizzle with olive oil just before eating.

たたききゅうりの酢じょうゆ漬け
Easy pickled cucumber

[Serves 4]

100 ml soy sauce

100 ml vinegar

4 tbsp sugar

6 mini cucumbers

1–2 red chillies, chopped

2.5 cm piece of fresh
   root ginger

See photograph on page 103

1. Combine the soy sauce, vinegar and sugar together in a bowl.

2. Trim the ends of the cucumbers and bash them with a rolling pin until they crack. Cut each cucumber into 4–6 pieces.

3. Put the cucumbers and chopped chillies into a plastic food bag and add the soy sauce mixture prepared in step 1. Seal and leave to marinate in the refrigerator for at least 2–3 hours.

4. Peel the ginger and chop it finely into matchsticks.

5. Tip the cucumbers and chillies into a serving bowl. Scatter with the ginger just before serving.

たたききゅうりの
酢じょうゆ漬け
Easy pickled cucumber

_____

This small side dish is always
the most popular among my
family, even when there are
other delicacies on the table.
This can be eaten on the day
it is made, but the flavour
improves over the following days.
So make plenty and enjoy over
several days!

ごちそう豆腐

Gochiso-dofu (decorated tofu)

This *gochiso-dofu* is made with all kinds of ingredients cut into small pieces, each with different textures or tastes. Toppings on tofu are usually leftovers from my fridge. This is a very convenient and impressive-looking dish when we have unexpected guests.

To achieve the neat appearance of this dish, it is important to pay attention to details such as wrapping the tofu with kitchen paper to absorb the excess water, extending the kitchen paper above the tofu so the toppings don't fall off, and pouring the sauce, little by little, along the edge of the tofu.

ご ち そ う 豆 腐

Gochiso-dofu (decorated tofu)

[Serves 2~4]

1 pack silken tofu (about 350g)

2 slices of ham (or use roast beef, roast chicken or canned tuna)

20g fresh root ginger, peeled

3 tbsp chopped spring onion

5 shiso leaves or a mix of mint and basil leaves

handful of peanuts

handful of white sesame seeds

[sauce]

5cm square of kombu kelp

50ml mirin

150ml soy sauce

See photograph on page 104

1. Make the sauce: rinse the kombu lightly and wipe with kitchen paper. Put the mirin in a small saucepan and bring to the boil. Boil it for 1–2 minutes, then turn off the heat and immediately add the soy sauce and kombu. Let it stand for at least 1 hour and then remove the kombu.

2. Drain the tofu and place on a serving plate. Wrap a folded piece of kitchen paper around the sides of the tofu to absorb excess water, making sure the edge of the kitchen paper extends 2cm above the tofu. Place in the refrigerator to chill the tofu thoroughly.

3. Prepare your toppings (ham, ginger, spring onions, shiso and peanuts), making sure they are all cut into small even-sized pieces.

4. Pile the toppings onto the chilled tofu. Sprinkle with sesame seeds and remove the kitchen paper.

5. Pour the sauce little by little along the edge of the tofu so that it doesn't disturb the beautifully arranged toppings.

いんげんと豚ひき肉の香味炒め
Stir-fried green beans and minced pork

[Serves 4]

400g fine green beans

1 tbsp vegetable oil

½ baby leek or ½ Japanese
leek or 1 spring onion,
finely chopped

2 tbsp finely chopped
fresh root ginger

1 tbsp finely
chopped garlic

150g minced pork

1 tbsp *shokoshu*
(Chinese sake), or use
Japanese sake

4 tbsp soy sauce

1–2 red chillies, finely chopped

1 tbsp sesame oil

See photograph on page 109

1. Cook the beans in boiling water until just
   tender. Rinse under cold running water. Pat
   dry and cut diagonally in half.
2. Heat the oil in a frying pan. Add the leek
   or spring onion, ginger and garlic and stir-
   fry until they release their aromas. Add the
   minced pork and continue to stir-fry.
3. When the pork is cooked, add the *shokoshu*
   and beans and stir-fry until heated through.
   Add the soy sauce and red chillies and mix
   thoroughly. Finish by drizzling with the
   sesame oil.

いんげんと豚ひき肉の
香味炒め
Stir-fried green beans
and minced pork

I often cook this dish – it was one of
my husband's favourites. Instead of
beans, you can also use aubergines,
green peppers or mangetout.

Sometimes I end up with leftover
fried pork mince on my plate after
I have eaten the beans, in which
case I tip it on top of a bowl of plain
steamed white rice or add it to
ramen noodles or fried rice.

豆腐ラザニア
Tofu lasagne

Lasagne is traditionally made with sheets of pasta,
however, I use tofu or aubergine instead. You may think
making lasagne is time consuming, but this recipe shows
that you can make it easily using double cream instead of
white sauce. Please put plenty of cheese on top!

豆腐ラザニア

Tofu lasagne

[Serves 4]

2 packs silken tofu
(about 700g)

2 tbsp olive oil

400ml meat sauce (see the
recipe opposite or use
shop-bought)

50ml double cream

150g grated Cheddar cheese

salt and pepper, to taste

See photograph on page 111

1. Wrap the tofu in kitchen paper and leave for about 15 minutes to absorb the excess water. Then cut each piece into five slices.

2. Put the olive oil into a frying pan and place over a medium heat. Working in batches, add the tofu slices and season with salt and pepper. Brown the tofu slowly on both sides, then remove from the pan.

3. Preheat the oven to 230°C, Gas Mark 8.

4. Spread a thin layer of meat sauce on the bottom of an ovenproof dish. Add a layer of tofu on top. Pour over half the cream, then repeat with another layer of meat sauce, tofu and cream. Sprinkle the grated cheese on top.

5. Bake in the oven for 15–20 minutes.

ミートソース

Meat sauce

[Serves 4]

50g bacon

1 onion

½ small carrot

½ celery stick

100g mushrooms

2 tbsp olive oil

1 garlic clove, finely chopped

500g mix of minced beef and
   minced pork

100ml red wine

290g pouch demi-glace
   concentrated meat stock

200ml tomato juice

1 tbsp Worcestershire sauce

2 tbsp tomato ketchup

salt and pepper, to taste

1. Finely chop the bacon.
2. Cut the onion, carrot and celery into small dice and chop the mushrooms.
3. Heat the olive oil in a frying pan over a medium heat and stir-fry the garlic and bacon. Add the minced meat and stir-fry until browned. Season with salt and pepper and stir in the onion, carrot and celery. Add the mushrooms and stir-fry.
4. Pour in the red wine and let it come to the boil. Add the demi-glace stock and tomato juice, then reduce the heat and simmer for 20–25 minutes. Add the Worcestershire sauce, ketchup and more salt and pepper, to taste.

甘辛粉吹きいも

Kofuki-imo
(salty-sweet potatoes)

When I first served this dish to my British friends in the UK, I remember everyone was very surprised. This potato recipe, cooked with soy sauce and sugar, was totally unfamiliar to them. But they all loved it. The scoop of butter that I add at the end, just before serving, is essential to give it a rich flavour.

甘辛粉吹きいも

Kofuki-imo (salty-sweet potatoes)

[Serves 4]

3 tbsp sugar

2 tbsp soy sauce

4 potatoes (600g)

20g butter

See photograph on page 115

1. Combine the sugar and soy sauce in a bowl and mix well until the sugar dissolves.

2. Peel and quarter the potatoes. Put them into a saucepan, cover with water and place over a high heat. When it comes to the boil, cover with a lid, reduce the heat and simmer for 10–15 minutes until tender.

3. Drain the potatoes well, tip back into the pan and place over the heat again to dry them thoroughly. Add the sugar and soy sauce mixture and stir briskly to coat the potatoes with the sauce. Add the butter and toss the potatoes until they are coated, then remove from the heat and serve.

長ねぎとじゃがいものグラタン
Leek and potato gratin

[Serves 4]

3 potatoes (400g)

2–3 anchovy fillets

2 baby leeks or 2 Japanese
leeks or 4 spring onions

200ml double cream

150–200g grated Cheddar
cheese

salt and pepper, to taste

See photograph on page 118

1. Preheat the oven to 220–230°C, Gas Mark
   7–8.

2. Peel the potatoes and slice them into 5mm
   round slices or half-moons (*hangetsu-giri*,
   see pages 228–230). Soak in cold water
   and drain well.

3. Place a few pieces of kitchen paper in an
   ovenproof dish. Arrange the potatoes on it
   in an even layer, cover loosely with clingfilm
   and microwave for 6–8 minutes until soft.
   Remove the clingfilm and kitchen paper.

4. Tear the anchovies into small pieces. Cut the
   leeks or spring onions into 5cm long pieces
   and thinly slice lengthways.

5. Arrange the anchovies and leeks or spring
   onions between the layers of potatoes.

6. Season the double cream with salt and pepper
   and pour evenly over the potatoes. Sprinkle
   the top with cheese and bake in the oven for
   20–25 minutes.

長ねぎとじゃがいものグラタン
Leek and potato gratin

I have been cooking this gratin for more than 30 years now and this was one of my husband's favourites. Instead of white sauce, I simply pour double cream over the ingredients and bake it in the oven. The important point is to cook the potatoes in the microwave first so that they are tender. It may look difficult, but in fact this dish is very easy. Please try it for yourself.

野 菜 の 揚 げ び た し
Deep-fried vegetables in *mentsuyu*

I enjoy making various different sauces in my kitchen, but *mentsuyu* (a broth for noodles) comes in especially handy because it can be used for so many dishes; it's good for noodles as well as simmered dishes, or *donburi* (rice topped with meat or vegetables, and sauce) and can be cooked and stored in the refrigerator. For this recipe, you can substitute lotus root, or various types of potato for the vegetables.

野 菜 の 揚 げ び た し

Deep-fried vegetables in *mentsuyu*

[Serves 4]

3 aubergines

⅛ pumpkin (*kabocha* squash)

4 green asparagus spears

½ red pepper

½ yellow pepper

50g fine green beans

400ml *mentsuyu* (see page 183)

vegetable oil, for deep-frying

See photograph on page 121

1. Remove the stems of the aubergines and cut them in half lengthways, then cut each half into 4 pieces. Soak the aubergines in water for about 5 minutes, then pat dry.

2. Remove the seeds of the pumpkin and cut into bite-sized chunks, about 1.5cm thick. Place some kitchen paper on a microwave-proof plate, put the pumpkin pieces on top and microwave at 600W for 1–2 minutes.

3. Cut off the woody stems of the asparagus and cut each spear diagonally into 4 pieces.

4. Halve the peppers, remove the seeds and core and slice into thin strips. Cut the beans diagonally in half.

5. Put the mentsuyu in a shallow dish.

6. Heat the oil for deep-frying in a large saucepan. Deep-fry all the vegetables for a few minutes and drain on kitchen paper, then transfer to the dish of mentsuyu while they are still hot.

7. Serve hot or cold. You can keep the vegetables in the refrigerator for 2–3 days.

お弁当 I Bento (box lunch)

お弁当

Bento (box lunch)

The Japanese bento, or lunch box, is traditionally tightly packed with colourful foods and rice. It has fascinated many people overseas, who find it fun and exciting to see what's inside a bento box and the name 'bento' has now become widely acknowledged throughout the world.

I started making bento for my children when they entered kindergarten and continued for 14 years until they graduated from high school. Looking back, I realise that I learned a lot through bento making. 'What's the best way to pack it?', 'How can I make one that they would love?' I was constantly thinking these thoughts and I tried different methods on a daily basis to make a bento box that had a good balance of flavour and colour, as well as looked appetising.

As mornings are always busy, I have developed time-saving and efficient preparation techniques, such as making side dishes in advance and storing them in the refrigerator or preparing a bento box while making dinner the night before. I've realised that after all these years of putting a lot of effort into making bento, it has made me better at cooking.

There are no rules for making bento. If you find a recipe you like in this book, start by putting it into your bento. You will soon find your favourite bento recipes.

日本の料理道具
Japanese cooking utensils

【巻きす】
Makisu

【盤台・しゃもじ】
Handai and Shamoji

【おろし金】
Oroshigane

【ごまいり】
Goma-iri

【 菜箸・盛りつけ箸 】
Saibashi and Moritsuke-bashi

【 土鍋 】
Donabe

【 蒸し器 】
Mushiki

日本の料理道具
Japanese cooking utensils

There are many different kinds of utensils for Japanese cooking. Each is made with great attention to detail by the hands of Japanese artisans, and the more I use them, the more I am impressed with how practical they are. Every time I use these tools, I feel a sense of appreciation towards all the craftsmen and women throughout Japan.

【巻きす】
Makisu (rolling mat)

Mainly used for making sushi rolls, these are made of bamboo. They can also be used to form *tamago-yaki* (rolled Japanese omelettes) or to squeeze out excess water from boiled vegetables, etc.

【盤台・しゃもじ】
Handai
(wooden sushi tub, wide cooking bowl)
Shamoji (rice paddle)

Tools used for making sushi rice. They absorb the excess water to help make delicious sushi rice.

【おろし金】
Oroshigane (grater)

There are various types of graters in Japan. The grater on the left is called *oni-oroshi*, and it is used for coarsely grating daikon. By grating coarsely, loss of moisture is kept to a minimum. The grater in the centre is made of copper, handmade by craftsmen. The grater on the right is made from shark skin and is exclusively used for grating wasabi. By using this, you can make airy and creamy grated wasabi.

【ごまいり】
Goma-iri
(sesame seed toaster)

A utensil specifically for toasting sesame seeds. You can use a dry frying pan instead, but this tool means you can toast sesame seeds without burning them, which enhances their fragrance.

【菜箸・盛りつけ箸】
Saibashi Moritsuke-bashi
(cooking chopsticks and serving chopsticks)

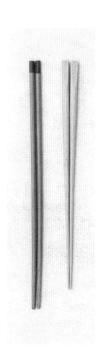

These chopsticks are not used for eating, but for cooking or serving a meal. *Saibashi* is used for stir-frying and for cooking in general. *Moritsuke-bashi* is used exclusively for serving. The narrow end has a sharp point, enabling you to pick up even the smallest items. The opposite end is slanted, so it can be used like a spatula or to pick up soft items without squashing them.

【土鍋】
Donabe (Japanese clay pot)

This is a ceramic pot that is often used for making hot pot dishes, but because of its excellent heat retention, it is quite versatile. I use it for cooking rice, simmering dishes and so on.

【蒸し器】
Mushiki (steamer)

Many Japanese dishes involve steaming, so the steamer is an important cooking tool. The steamer enhances the flavour of vegetables and gives dishes a mild taste.

すり鉢
Mortar

Mortars vary in size, from small to large. My mother often made dishes with sesame seeds in, so I have been grinding sesame seeds in a mortar since I was little. This mortar is the one my mother used. It has been in use for such a long time that it has cracks in it.

There are ready-made sesame pastes available in stores, but nothing compares to a homemade paste using a mortar. I intend to pass this mortar to my children one day, just as my mother passed it on to me. I hope it will remind them of me when they use it someday.

3

ご飯もの、麺、その他

RICE, NOODLES
& MORE

牛丼

Gyudon (beef on rice)

Gyudon is one of the most popular fast foods in Japan. The main ingredients are onion and beef, so making this outside of Japan is easy. Even inexpensive cuts of beef can taste delicious when cooked in white wine.

牛 丼

Gyudon (beef on rice)

[Serves 4]

4 onions

500g thinly sliced beef

200ml water

400ml white wine

150ml soy sauce

100ml mirin

4 tbsp sugar

cooked rice, to serve

red pickled ginger, to garnish

See photograph on page 134

1. Slice the onions into 1cm thick half-moons (*hangetsu-giri*, see pages 228–230).
2. Cut the beef into 6–7cm lengths.
3. Heat the water and white wine in a saucepan over a medium heat. When it comes to the boil, add the beef. Return to the boil, then skim the surface of the broth. Turn the heat to low and simmer for 10–15 minutes. If the beef is still tough, simmer it a little longer.
4. Add the soy sauce, mirin and sugar and cover the pan with a drop-lid. Simmer for a further 10 minutes.
5. Add the onions and simmer until they are translucent. Turn off the heat and let it stand.
6. Serve the beef along with the sauce on top of freshly cooked rice. Garnish with a little red pickled ginger.

しょうがご飯

Ginger rice

[Serves 4]

400g rice

30g fresh root ginger

2 pieces *abura-age* (thinly sliced deep-fried tofu, shop-bought)

2 tbsp light soy sauce

1 tbsp mirin

1 tbsp sake

about 400ml dashi (see page 19)

salt, to taste

See photograph on page 138

1. Wash the rice well and drain. Let it stand for 10–15 minutes.
2. Peel and finely chop the ginger.
3. Pour hot water over the *abura-age* to remove any excess oil, squeeze lightly and pat dry. Cut it into 5mm squares.
4. Combine the light soy sauce, mirin and sake in a jug and add enough dashi to make 400ml sauce.
5. Put the rice into a heavy-based saucepan. Add the *abura-age* and dashi mixture.
6. Cover with a lid and place over a high heat. When it comes to the boil, turn down the heat and simmer for 10–12 minutes. Turn off the heat and let it stand for about 10 minutes to allow the rice to settle, then mix in the ginger. Season to taste with a little salt if necessary.

しょうがご飯

Ginger rice

The ginger is not cooked with the rice, but is added after cooking. By doing this, the aroma of the ginger is stronger. I often eat this dish with some crispy crumbled nori seaweed.

親子丼

Chicken and egg on rice

―――――――――――――――――

Have you ever experienced a sudden intense craving for a certain dish? For me, *oyako-don* (chicken and egg on rice) is one such dish. This recipe is so easy – whenever I feel like eating it, I know I can prepare it right away because I always have some chicken in my freezer.

To keep the smooth and soft texture of egg, which is very important, turn off the heat after adding the egg and put a lid on the pan to half-cook the egg in the residual heat.

親 子 丼

Chicken and egg on rice

[Serves 2]

½ onion

1 boneless skin-on chicken
thigh (about 200g)

4 eggs

chopped *mitsuba* or parsley,
to garnish

cooked rice, nori seaweed and
pickles, to serve

[dashi mixture]

100 ml dashi (see page 19)

3 tbsp soy sauce

2 tbsp sugar

2 tbsp mirin

1. Thickly slice the onion and cut the chicken
into small, bite-sized pieces.

2. Combine the ingredients for the dashi mixture.

3. Beat 2 eggs in one bowl and 2 eggs in a
separate bowl.

4. Put half of the dashi mixture into a saucepan
and bring to the boil. Add half the chicken
pieces and cook for a few minutes, then add
half the onion slices and simmer for 1–2
minutes.

5. While it is simmering, take one of the bowls of
beaten egg and pour two-thirds into the pan,
then cover with a lid. When it is half-cooked,
pour the remaining one-third of the beaten
egg evenly around the rim of the pan. Turn off
the heat, add the *mitsuba* and allow to settle
with the lid on. (The egg should be slightly
runny.) Repeat the process to make a second
serving.

6. Serve the chicken and egg on top of plain
steamed white rice in individual bowls. Serve
with some nori seaweed and pickles.

豚 肉 と 野 菜 の
炊 き 込 み ご 飯

Steamed rice with pork and
vegetables

Sometimes I just want to eat a light *takikomi gohan* (rice steamed with vegetables, meat or fish). However, this recipe has a rich intense flavour. The meat should be well seasoned so that its 'umami' flavour can soak into the rice during cooking. As this recipe uses soybeans as well as meat, it is hearty and filling.

豚肉と野菜の炊き込みご飯
Steamed rice with pork and vegetables

[Serves 4]

400g rice

150g sliced pork

½ carrot

2–3 fresh shiitake
mushrooms

200g cooked soybeans

1 tbsp soy sauce

1 tbsp mirin

1 tbsp sake

about 400ml dashi
(see page 19)

salt, to taste

[marinade for pork]

2 tbsp soy sauce

½ tbsp sugar

1 tsp ginger juice (from
grated fresh root ginger)

See photograph on page 145

1. Wash the rice and drain in a sieve. Let it stand for 10–15 minutes.

2. Chop the pork into tiny pieces and marinate in the soy sauce, sugar and ginger juice.

3. Peel the carrot and cut into small quarter-rounds (*icho-giri*, see pages 228–230). Cut off the stems of the shiitake mushrooms and cut into 2cm squares.

4. Put the rice in a saucepan and scatter over the carrot, shiitake mushrooms and soybeans. Top with the marinated pork.

5. Pour the soy sauce, mirin and sake into a measuring jug. Add enough dashi to make it up to 400ml and season with salt. Gently pour the dashi mixture on to the rice around the edge of the pan. Cover with a lid and place over a high heat. When it comes to the boil, turn the heat down to low and cook for 10–12 minutes.

6. When the rice is cooked, turn off the heat and let it stand for about 10 minutes. Stir the rice well before serving.

レンジ赤飯

Sekihan (adzuki beans and rice)

[Serves 4]

60g dried adzuki beans

400g *mochigome* (glutinous rice)

salt, to taste

roasted black sesame seeds, to serve

See photograph on page 148

1. Soak the adzuki beans in plenty of cold water for 2–3 hours.

2. Rinse the glutinous rice and soak in water for about 30 minutes, then drain.

3. Drain the adzuki beans and put into a saucepan with 300ml water. Place the pan over a low heat and simmer for about 1 hour until the beans are barely cooked.

   * Make sure some firmness remains (if you can crush the beans with your fingers, they are overcooked).

4. Drain the adzuki beans in a sieve, saving the water they were cooked in. Add more cold water until it measures 300ml. Set aside and leave to cool.

5. Put the adzuki beans, rice and measured liquid into a microwave-proof bowl and cover it loosely with clingfilm. Microwave on 600W for about 9 minutes.

6. Remove from the microwave and stir well. Cover the bowl with clingfilm once again and microwave for a further 2–3 more minutes.

7. Place in a serving bowl, season with salt and sprinkle with sesame seeds.

レンジ赤飯

Sekihan
(adzuki beans and rice)

Sekihan is usually served at special occasions in Japan, but I often cook it regardless of occasion as I love it. Traditionally, *sekihan* is cooked in a steamer, but I came up with the idea to use a microwave.

The *sekihan* can become a little bit too soft depending on the power of your microwave, so please use the cooking times given here as a guide and adjust as needed.

三 色 丼

Three-colour rice bowl

This is a typical Japanese home-cooked dish that is served in many Japanese households. Here, I've given the recipe that my mother taught me. I cook the minced chicken briefly in a pan and use the broth it was simmered in to cook the rice, which provides plenty of flavour.

This method takes a little time and effort, but it adds depth to the taste and I like it this way. Make sure you top the rice with plenty of thinly sliced mangetout.

三色丼

Three-colour rice bowl

[Serves 4]

about 400ml dashi
(see page 19)

4 tbsp soy sauce

2 tbsp sake

3 tbsp mirin

300g minced chicken

2 cups rice, washed and
drained (see page 12)

1½–2 tbsp sugar

100g mangetout

salt, to taste

[scrambled eggs]

4 eggs

1½–2 tbsp sugar

2 tbsp sake

[garnish]

nori seaweed

red pickled ginger

See photograph on page 150

1. Put 200ml dashi into a saucepan with 1
   tablespoon of the soy sauce, 1 tablespoon
   of the sake and 1 tablespoon of the mirin.
   Bring to the boil, then add the minced chicken
   and reduce the heat to a simmer. When the
   chicken is cooked, strain and save the broth.

2. Put the broth into a measuring jug and add
   more dashi until it measures 400ml. Season
   with a little salt.

3. Put the rice in a rice cooker with the dashi
   broth. Turn on the rice cooker.*

   * If you don't have a rice cooker, see page 12.

4. Combine the remaining soy sauce, sake and
   mirin in another saucepan and add the sugar,
   then bring to the boil. Add the cooked chicken
   and simmer until the liquid is almost gone.

5. Make the scrambled eggs: beat the eggs in a
   bowl. Add the sugar and sake, season with a
   little salt and mix together. Pour the egg into
   a saucepan and place over a medium heat.
   When the egg just starts to set around the
   edges, reduce the heat and stir the mixture
   with 4 chopsticks until it is cooked.

6. Blanch the mangetout and refresh in cold
   water. Drain and cut diagonally into thin strips.

7. Divide the rice between serving bowls.
   Arrange the chicken, scrambled eggs and
   mangetout on top. Garnish with some nori and
   red pickled ginger.

ビーフカレー

Beef curry

[Serves 4]

4 onions

2 carrots

4 potatoes

1 kg beef chuck steak

4 tbsp vegetable oil

1 tsp cumin seeds

1 tbsp grated garlic

1 tbsp grated fresh root
ginger

3 tbsp curry powder

1 tsp each of garam masala,
ground turmeric, ground
coriander

seeds from 5 cardamom
pods, ground

1.2 litres water

3 tbsp flour

2 tomatoes

3 tbsp tomato ketchup

1 tbsp Worcestershire sauce
(or *tonkatsu* sauce)

salt and pepper, to taste

cooked rice, to serve

fukujinzuke pickles,
to garnish (optional)

*See photograph on page
154*

1. Thinly slice the onions. Peel the carrots and slice into 2 cm-thick rounds or half-moons. Peel and quarter the potatoes, then soak in cold water and drain well.

2. Cut the beef into 4 cm cubes.

3. Heat half the vegetable oil in a large saucepan over a low heat, add the cumin seeds and stir-fry until fragrant. Add the onion and stir-fry over a medium-high heat to cook off the moisture, then lower the heat and continue to stir-fry until golden brown. Add the garlic and ginger and stir-fry. Add the curry powder and other ground spices and stir-fry until they become fragrant. Add the water and stir to combine.

4. Dust the beef cubes with 1 teaspoon of salt and a small amount of pepper, then toss in the flour.

5. Heat the remaining oil in a frying pan over a medium-high heat and sear the beef in batches. When browned, add them to the saucepan with the spices. Bring to the boil, then skim the surface. Put on a lid, reduce the heat and simmer for 30–40 minutes.

6. When the beef is tender, roughly chop the tomatoes and add them to the pan. Add the carrots and potatoes and simmer for another 10–15 minutes. When cooked through, add the ketchup and Worcestershire sauce and season with salt and pepper to taste.

7. Serve the beef curry on top of cooked rice in bowls. Garnish with *fukujinzuke* pickles.

ビーフカレー

Beef curry

Curry with rice is one of the three most popular Japanese home-cooked meals. It is common to make it with shop-bought curry paste, but in this recipe I show you how to make your own using various spices. The sweetness of the onions and the flavour of the meat are key in this dish, so make sure you stir-fry the onions thoroughly to draw out their natural sweetness.

カ ツ 丼

Katsu-don (breaded pork on rice)

This small frying pan with a handle is made specifically for cooking katsu-don or *oyako-don* (see page 140). My mother used this before I was born and I use it to this day. It's a good size for cooking just enough for one *donburi* bowl, and is designed to make it easy to pour the contents of the pan directly over a serving of rice.

カツ丼

Katsu-don (breaded pork on rice)

[Serves 1]

1 breaded pork fillet
(see *tonkatsu*, page 55)

¼ onion

2 eggs

100 ml dashi (see page 19)

1 tbsp sugar

2 tbsp soy sauce

1 tbsp mirin

cooked rice, to serve

1. Cut the breaded pork into bite-sized pieces.

2. Thinly slice the onion.

3. Beat the eggs.

4. Combine the dashi, sugar, soy sauce and mirin in a small frying pan with a lid. Place it over a medium heat and add the sliced onion. Simmer for a few minutes, then add the breaded pork and continue cooking for a few more minutes. When it comes to the boil, pour the beaten eggs over the pork, cover with the lid and cook for 1 minute more until cooked but still runny.

5. Put the cooked rice in a bowl and tip the contents of the pan over the top.

ちらしずし
Chirashi-zushi

I cook various kinds of sushi throughout the year. But in the Hinamatsuri (Doll Festival) season in early March, I always make *chirashi-zushi*. If you don't have all the ingredients listed, don't worry too much. But please do make the *kinshi-tamago* (shredded egg omelettes) to serve with this. Thinly shred the omelette, loosen the shreds and scatter them on top of the rice. This makes the dish look gorgeous. It can take some practice to make really thin omelettes, but it's easy once you know how.

ちらしずし
Chirashi-zushi

[Serves 4]

[sushi rice]

400g rice

400ml water

100ml vinegar

1½–2 tbsp sugar

1 tsp salt

[sweet simmered
  shiitake muhrooms]

8 dried shiitake mushrooms

100ml dashi (see page 19)

2 tbsp sugar

1½ tbsp soy sauce

1 tbsp sake

1 tbsp mirin

[vinegared lotus root]

1 lotus root (200g)

5 tbsp vinegar

2 tbsp sugar

salt

*See photographs on pages
  162–5*

1. Make the sushi rice: rinse the rice and drain it in a sieve. Let it stand for about 15 minutes. Put the rice into a saucepan, add the water to the pan and cook (see page 12).

2. Meanwhile, combine the vinegar, sugar and salt in a bowl and stir to dissolve. Pour this sushi vinegar over the freshly cooked rice and fold it in as the rice cools.

3. Make the sweet simmered shiitake mushrooms: soak the shiitake mushrooms in water until they become soft. Lightly squeeze them to remove the water and cut off the stems. Combine the dashi with the other ingredients in a saucepan and bring to the boil. Add the shiitake mushrooms, cover with a drop-lid and simmer over a low heat for 10–15 minutes until the liquid is reduced. Turn off the heat and let it stand for a while to let the mushrooms absorb the sauce. When cool, cut the mushrooms into quarters.

4. Make the vinegared lotus root: peel and cut the lotus root into 1cm-thick quarter-rounds (*icho-giri*, see pages 228–230). Soak in water and drain well. Combine the vinegar, sugar and a little salt in a pan and bring to the boil. Add the lotus root and simmer for 1–2 minutes over a medium heat while stirring quickly. Allow to cool.

Continued overleaf

ちらしずし
Chirashi-zushi

[Serves 4]

[*kinshi-tamago*
  (shredded egg crepe)]
2 eggs
1 tbsp sugar
½ tbsp sake
salt

vegetable oil

[sashimi]
1 *saku* block
  tuna (lean)
1 *saku* block
  white-flesh fish
  (sea bream etc.)
1 leg cooked octopus

sudachi,
  pickled ginger,
  crumbled nori seaweed
  --- for garnish

soy sauce,
  grated wasabi
  --- for sashimi

5. Make the kinshi-tamago (shredded egg crepes): beat the eggs in a bowl, add the sugar, sake and salt, mix well then strain. Using kitchen paper, grease a small frying pan with some vegetable oil. Heat the pan over a low heat. Pour a small amount of egg mixture into the pan and spread it out to make a thin layer. Before the egg starts to brown, flip it over and cook the other side. Remove the egg crepe from the pan. Repeat the same processs with the remaining egg mixture. Stack up the egg crepes, roll them together and slice them into thin strips. Loosen them gently by pulling them apart.

6. Cut the sashimi into 1.5-2 cm cubes.

7. Serve the sushi rice onto a plate or in a bento box and top with plenty of kinshi-tamago. Scatter diced sashimi, sweet simmered shiitake mushrooms and vinegared lotus root on top. Garnish with sudachi, pickled ginger to taste and top with crumbled nori seaweed. Serve wasabi and soy sauce with the sashimi.

裏 巻 き ず し

Uramaki-zushi (inside-out sushi rolls)

───────────────

I often make this dish when I am abroad. The trick is to be sure to add the fillings in the correct order: first the avocado, then the shiso leaves, mayonnaise and crab sticks. This way the colours will look beautiful.

裏 巻 き ず し

Uramaki-zushi (inside-out sushi rolls)

[Makes 36 pieces]

3 sheets nori seaweed

1–1½ avocados

9 shiso leaves or a mix of basil and mint leaves

mayonnaise, to taste

18 crab sticks

toasted white sesame seeds, to coat

[sushi rice]

400g rice

400ml water

100ml rice vinegar

1½–2 tbsp sugar

1 tsp salt

1. Make the sushi rice according to the instructions on page 161.

2. Cut the nori seaweed sheets in half. Cut squares of greaseproof paper that are slightly larger than the nori sheets.

3. Peel and stone the avocados and cut into even-sized strips. Cut the shiso leaves in half, if using.

4. Place the paper on to a *makisu* (rolling mat). Place the nori on top and spread a layer of sushi rice over it. Using the paper, turn the noriand rice over, so that the nori side faces upwards.

5. A little below the centre of the nori sheet, make a thin line of avocado strips. Place 3 shiso leaves on top and spread 1 teaspoon of mayonnaise thinly over them. Then place 3 crab sticks on top.

6. Roll up the *makisu* over the ingredients, pressing it gently. Continue rolling to the edge, making sure you don't roll up the paper in the sushi. Press lightly again, sealed side down, and remove the *makisu* and the paper.

7. Coat the sushi rolls with sesame seeds. Cut each roll into 6 pieces. Repeat to make more sushi rolls.

大切にしたい日本の手仕事　漆<ruby>漆<rt>うるし</rt></ruby>

Urushi lacquerware:
a Japanese handicraft
that should be cherished

Urushi

In Japan, there are various *shikki* (lacquerware goods) such as *owan* (wooden bowls), chopsticks, *jubako* (multi-tiered boxes), *chataku* (Japanese teacup saucers), *shuki* (sake cups) and many others. Making urushi lacquerware is a traditional Japanese craft and one of the symbols of Japan. People often think that urushi lacquerware is mainly used for special occasions such as New Year. However, my mother loved urushi lacquerware so, in my parents' house we used it every day, as bowls for miso soup and as lunch boxes.

The lacquered soup bowl with my name on it is one that I have been using since childhood and it is my pride and joy. The more I appreciate the beauty of urushi lacquerware, the more I love it; I visit urushi lacquerware craftsmen's workshops or create urushi lacquerware which I design myself. I now have quite a collection.

Urushi lacquerware is very delicate so it needs to be appropriately cared for, washed gently and thoroughly wiped dry. But, if you use it carefully, it will last a lifetime. Besides being beautiful, it is functional in keeping warm food warm and cold food cold. These days, however, urushi lacquerware is rarely used by the younger generation. I feel sad that these works of traditional Japanese craftsmanship are starting to disappear from our daily lives.

Beautiful and functional tools can make our life happier. I do hope that people begin to realise the beauty and functionality of urushi lacquerware and start to use it again. We should never lose the skills required to make this traditional Japanese craft, so that it can be handed down to the next generation.

Urushi lacquer lunch box. It can be used as a lunch box or, when separated, as a pair of serving dishes.

だしみつ卵

Sweet dashi omelette

This recipe looks simple, but requires a little practice in getting the cooking temperature just right. I use a square frying pan especially for making rolled omelettes, but you can use a regular frying pan if you don't mind a round shape. Even if the layers don't line up during the process, there's no need to worry. If you can roll the last layer neatly, it will be a success.

だしみつ卵

Sweet dashi omelette

[Makes 1 omelette]

6 eggs

vegetable oil, for frying

[sweet dashi sauce]

100 ml dashi (see page 19)

40 g sugar

1 tsp light soy sauce

salt

See photograph on page 175

1. Make the sweet dashi sauce: warm the dashi gently in a saucepan, add the sugar and stir until dissolved. Add the light soy sauce, season with salt and allow to cool.
2. Beat the eggs in a bowl. Add the sweet dashi sauce, mix well and strain.
3. Place an omelette pan over a medium heat and use kitchen paper to grease it with vegetable oil.
4. Pour a little egg mixture into the pan. Quickly pull it towards the edge of the pan while it is still half-cooked to create a centre roll. If you need to add more oil to the pan, repeat the process in step 3. Add a little more egg mixture into the pan making sure that it flows under the centre roll as well. Roll it towards the edge of the pan. Repeat this several times.
5. When it is done, allow to cool and cut it into bite-sized pieces.

なすのドライカレー

Curried rice with aubergine and pickled eggs

[Serves 4]

1 onion

2 green peppers

4–6 aubergines

vegetable oil for deep-frying, plus 2 tbsp

400g mix of minced beef and minced pork

2 tbsp curry powder

2 tbsp curry paste

ground spices, such as garam masala, ground turmeric, ground cumin and ground coriander (a good pinch of each)

1 tbsp tomato ketchup

1 tbsp *tonkatsu* sauce

salt and pepper, to taste

cooked rice, to serve

fukujinzuke pickles, to garnish (optional)

[pickled eggs]

6–8 eggs

2 tbsp soy sauce

1 tbsp vinegar

1 tsp sugar

See photograph on page 178

1. First make the pickled eggs: set a timer for 12 minutes. Put the eggs into a saucepan, cover with cold water and place over a high heat. When it comes to the boil, reduce the heat to medium-low. When the time is up, put the eggs into cold water, then peel and wipe off the excess water. Combine the soy sauce, vinegar and sugar in a plastic food bag and add the eggs. Drain the air from the bag, seal it and place in the refrigerator to marinate for 2–3 hours before eating.

2. Cut the onions into 1cm pieces.

3. Halve and deseed the green peppers, then chop them into 1cm pieces.

4. Trim the aubergines and cut into 2.5cm round slices. Soak them in water for a few minutes, then drain and pat dry. Heat the oil for deep-frying in a saucepan and deep-fry the aubergines until cooked through. Drain well.

5. Heat 2 tablespoons vegetable oil in another frying pan. Add the minced meat and stir-fry. When the meat is browned, add the onions and continue to stir-fry.

6. Add the curry powder, curry paste, ground spices, tomato ketchup and tonkatsu sauce. Stir in the green peppers, season with salt and pepper and add the fried aubergines.

7. Ladle the warm curry over freshly cooked rice. Add a halved pickled egg to each plate and garnish with *fukujinzuke*.

なすのドライカレー

Curried rice with aubergine and pickled eggs

———————————

Curried rice with aubergine has been my favourite recipe since my children were little. The natural sweetness of the aubergine comes out when it is fried. The pickled eggs that are served on the side are delicious on their own, so please try them. The eggs taste even better left in the refrigerator overnight to marinate, as they soak up all the flavours.

もやしとねぎのあえそば

Noodles with prawns and vegetables

This is one of my family's favourite easy-to-make dishes – it's good to have the garlic and ginger soy sauce to hand as it can be used for cooking a variety of dishes, including fried rice. The added coriander leaves and Szechuan peppercorns give the dish an authentic Chinese taste, and make it surprisingly delicious.

もやしとねぎのあえそば

Noodles with prawns and vegetables

[Serves 4]

150 g raw, shelled prawns

2 baby leeks or 2 Japanese leeks or 4 spring onions

2 portions steamed Chinese noodles

½ tbsp oyster sauce

vegetable oil, for frying

½ tbsp *shokoshu* (Chinese sake), or use Japanese sake

1 pack bean sprouts

salt and pepper, to taste

sesame oil, to taste

[to serve]

ground Szechuan peppercorns

coriander leaves

chopped red chilli

vinegar

[garlic and ginger soy sauce]

2–3 garlic cloves

2.5 cm piece of fresh root ginger

400 ml soy sauce

See photograph on page 181

1. First make the garlic and ginger soy sauce: peel and thinly slice the garlic and ginger and place in a clean jam jar with the soy sauce. Set aside for 2–3 hours.

2. Rinse the prawns and devein them. Pat dry with kitchen paper.

3. Cut the leeks or spring onions into 5 cm-long pieces and then thinly slice lengthways.

4. Gently pull the noodles apart one by one to loosen them.

5. Combine 2 tablespoons of the garlic and ginger soy sauce with the oyster sauce in a bowl.

6. Heat ½ tablespoon oil in a frying pan and stir-fry the prawns. Add the *shokoshu* and season with salt and pepper. Remove from the pan as soon as the prawns are cooked.

7. Add 1 tablespoon oil to a wok or large frying pan and stir-fry the noodles over a high heat for a minute or two. Remove from the pan. Add another 1–2 tablespoons oil to the pan and stir-fry the bean sprouts and spring onion.

8. Return the prawns and noodles to the pan and stir. Turn off the heat and add the garlic and ginger soy sauce made in step 5 and toss together. Season with salt, pepper and sesame oil.

9. Pile on to a serving plate and sprinkle with ground Szechuan pepper and coriander leaves. Mix the chopped chilli with a little vinegar and serve with the noodles.

ざるそば
Zaru soba (cold soba noodles)

[Serves 2]

200g dried soba
   noodles

crumbled nori seaweed

1 quantity *mentsuyu*
   (see below)

grated wasabi

baby leek or Japanese leek
   or spring onion (chopped
   and soaked in water),
   to garnish

See photograph on page 184

1. Bring plenty of water to the boil and add the
   soba. Stir the noodles occasionally to prevent
   them from sticking together.

2. When the noodles are about to boil over, add
   200ml water and continue boiling until the
   noodles are cooked through.

3. Drain the noddles and rinse them well under
   cold running water, then drain thoroughly.

4. Put the noodles into serving bowls and sprinkle
   crumbled nori seaweed on top. Pour the chilled
   mentsuyu broth over the noodles and garnish
   with wasabi and leek or spring onion.

めんつゆ
Mentsuyu (noodle broth)

[Serves 2]

800ml water

300ml soy sauce

200ml mirin

40g sugar

50g bonito flakes

1. Combine the water, soy sauce and mirin in a
   saucepan. Stir in the sugar until dissolved.

2. Place over a medium-high heat and bring just
   to the boil, then add the bonito flakes, reduce
   the heat to low and simmer for a few minutes.
   Remove from the heat and let it stand until it
   cools slightly.

3. Strain through a sieve and chill in the
   refrigerator.

   * *Mentsuyu* keeps in the refrigerator for 4–5
   days.

ざるそば
'Zaru soba'
(cold soba noodles)

めんつゆ

Zaru soba (cold soba noodles) with *Mentsuyu* (noodle broth)

Soba noodles, boiled and rinsed under cold running water, served with *mentsuyu* with a garnish of spring onion, wasabi and crumbled nori seaweed. I like the simple style of this dish. My mother taught me this *mentsuyu* recipe – it can be used for many recipes including *donburi* (rice topped with meat or vegetables and sauce).

ギョーザ
Gyoza (Chinese dumplings)

Gyoza is one of my favourite recipes to make. There are
various fillings for gyoza, but this is my favourite. Adding
the flour–water mixture when cooking the gyoza creates
the crispy bottoms. These are best eaten as soon as they
are cooked. Enjoy them with plenty of ginger and soy sauce
with vinegar and chilli oil.

ギョーザ

Gyoza (Chinese dumplings)

[Makes 24]

150g Chinese cabbage

150g white cabbage

½ tbsp sesame oil, plus extra for drizzling

1 tbsp chopped garlic

150g minced pork

1 tbsp *shokoshu* (Chinese sake)

1 tsp Chinese soup paste or chicken bouillon powder dissolved in 1 tbsp hot water and cooled

3 spring onions or 50g *nira* (garlic chives), finely chopped

24 thin *gyoza* wrappers (dumpling wrappers)

1 tsp flour

100ml water

vegetable oil, for frying

salt and pepper, to taste

[to serve]

soy sauce

vinegar

chilli oil

finely sliced fresh root ginger

See photograph on page 187

1. Finely chop both types of cabbage and put into separate bowls. Sprinkle 1 teaspoon salt into each bowl. Mix both of them lightly and leave to stand for a while to release some moisture, then squeeze the water out.

2. Heat the sesame oil in a frying pan and fry the chopped garlic.

3. Put the minced pork in a bowl. Add the *shokoshu* and soup paste and mix. Follow with the fried garlic, along with the oil, then the Chinese cabbage, cabbage and spring onion or *nira* and mix. Season with salt and pepper. Cover with clingfilm and leave to stand for 30 minutes.

4. To make the gyoza: use a teaspoon to scoop some mixture on to a gyoza wrapper. Wet the edges with a little water, fold it over and pinch to seal. Repeat with the remaining filling and wrappers.

5. Dissolve the flour in the water.

6. Heat a frying pan and add some oil and pan-fry half the dumplings at a time. Arrange the dumplings in a circle and cook for a few minutes. Pour in half the flour–water mixture, cover with a lid and cook over a low-medium heat. When the water has almost evaporated, pour a little sesame oil around the dumplings and continue to cook until the bottoms turn crispy. Transfer to a plate and serve with soy sauce, vinegar, chilli oil and sliced ginger.

まぐろのクロスティーニ
Tuna crostini

[Serves 4]

1 small garlic clove

150 g sushi-grade fresh tuna
(lean meat or medium fatty
flesh)

2 tbsp soy sauce

2 tbsp sake

½ cucumber

8 –10 slices of baguette
(each 2 cm thick)

olive oil, for drizzling
(optional)

[avocado cream]

1 avocado

juice of 1 lemon

1 tbsp olive oil

salt and pepper, to taste

See photograph on page 190

1. Cut the garlic into thin slices.

2. Bring a saucepan of water to the boil, add the tuna and boil for 15 seconds. Take out the tuna and immediately soak in iced water to cool. When cooled, drain and wipe thoroughly with kitchen paper.

3. Combine the soy sauce with the sake in a plastic food container, add the tuna, top with the garlic slices and marinate in the refrigerator for 2–3 hours. Drain the tuna and cut into 5 mm-thick slices just before serving.

4. Halve and stone the avocado. Using a spoon, scoop out the flesh into a bowl and mash. Add the lemon juice and olive oil and mix. Season with salt and pepper.

5. Chop the cucumber in half, trim the end, then thinly slice the cucumber lengthways.

6. Preheat the grill and toast the baguette slices until golden brown and crisp. Spread avocado cream evenly over the surface of the crostini and lay cucumber slices on top. Top with the sliced tuna and garlic slices. Drizzle with olive oil, if liked.

まぐろのクロスティーニ
Tuna crostini

Soy-sauce-marinated tuna has been enjoyed in Japan since long ago. It's tasty on its own, but it also goes well with bread and avocado, so this recipe is a sort of Italian appetiser. Adding garlic to the marinade makes it especially savoury.

お好み焼き
Okonomiyaki
(Japanese pancakes)

Okonomiyaki (literally 'your favourite things grilled') is one of the Japanese dishes that foreign visitors love. You can use any ingredients you like in place of the squid, prawns or pork that I introduce here. If you microwave (at 200 W) the dried bonito flakes for about 5 minutes, they will become crispy and more flavourful. Sprinkle over the okonomiyaki and add a little red pickled ginger for a delicious treat.

お 好 み 焼 き
Okonomiyaki (Japanese pancakes)

[Serves 4]

1 squid body (120g)

15 raw prawns (150g)

200g sliced pork belly

3 cabbage leaves (150g)

2–3 tbsp red pickled ginger

50g chopped spring onion

2–3 tbsp *agedama* (leftover fried tempura bits)

vegetable oil, for frying

4 eggs

[pancake batter]

100g *yamaimo* yam

1 egg

200ml dashi (see page 19)

200g flour

[topping]

okonomiyaki sauce (a thick Worcestershire sauce)

mayonnaise

aonori (seaweed flakes)

dried bonito flakes

See photograph on page 193

1. Cut the squid into 2cm squares.
2. Remove any shells and tails from the prawns. Slice them horizontally in half. Devein them, and cut in half lengthways.
3. Cut the pork slices into 5cm strips.
4. Shred the cabbage. Chop the red ginger finely.
5. Make the batter: peel and grate the *yamaimo* and add to a bowl with the egg and dashi. Mix together, then add the flour and stir lightly.
6. Add the shredded cabbage, chopped spring onion, *agedama* and red ginger to the batter and stir to combine. Add the squid and prawns.
7. Heat a little oil in a frying pan. Pour in a quarter of the batter (for 1 serving). Put the pork slices on top and cook for 3–4 minutes. Flip the pancake over and cook for another 3–4 minutes.
8. Heat a little oil in another frying pan. Crack an egg into the pan. Stir the yolk lightly. Place the pancake made in step 7 on top of the egg, pork side down, and continue cooking.
9. Turn it over on to a serving plate and spread okonomiyaki sauce and mayonnaise on top. Sprinkle with *aonori* and bonito flakes. Make 3 more pancakes with the remaining batter in the same way.

こねないパン

No-knead bread

[makes 1 x 25cm boule]

300g bread
    flour, plus
    extra for
    dusting

2 tsp sugar

½ tsp salt

1 tsp fast-action
    dried yeast

200ml water
    (at room
    temperature)

*See photograph
    on page 197*

.

1. Put the bread flour into a bowl and add the sugar, salt and yeast separately in that order. Mix well. Pour in the room-temperature water and stir well with a wooden spoon until all the flour mixture is incorporated. Form into a ball in the bowl, cover with clingfilm and leave to rise for about 2 hours until about double the original size.

   * Cooler room temperatures, such as in winter, will mean that the rising time may be longer.

2. When the dough has risen, dust some flour between the dough and the bowl and use a dough scraper to remove the dough from the edges of the bowl. Hold the dough in both hands. Shape into a ball in your palms, then stretch it out and shape it into a ball again, while dusting with more flour. Repeat this process several times to knock out the air. Smooth out the surface and shape into a ball. Return the dough to the bowl seamside down, cover with clingfilm and leave to prove for about 1 hour.

3. Line a round 25cm ovenproof pot or casserole with baking paper. Repeat the process described in step 2 and shape the dough into a ball. Dust the surface with flour and place into the pot and put on the lid. Let it rest in the pot for another hour, until the dough rises to 1.5 times its size.

4. Preheat the oven to 200°C, Gas Mark 6.

5. Place the pot in the oven and bake for 30 minutes with the lid on. Remove the lid and bake for a further 30 minutes until the surface is golden brown. Remove from the oven and transfer the bread to a wire rack to cool. Enjoy fresh from the oven, with butter.

こ ね な い パ ン
No-knead bread

I love piping hot bread, fresh out of the oven. This is the advantage of baking your own bread. Even if it's not perfect, you can still enjoy eating a freshly baked loaf. This recipe is a bit time-consuming, but there's no need to knead, so it doesn't require special skills. Feel free to experiment with the recipe by adding different ingredients to the dough, such as cheese, raisins and nuts.

大根そば鍋
Daikon noodle pot

Shave daikon with a peeler into noodle-like strips. Put only the amount you wish to eat into the pan and serve hot. You can enjoy the texture of daikon if you don't let it sit for too long in the soup, but it also tastes good when it has been simmered well. It has a light flavour, so you can eat plenty of it without feeling heavy in the stomach.

大根そば鍋

Daikon noodle pot

[Serves 4]

20cm piece of daikon
  (about 500g)

3 bundles of watercress

300–400g sliced pork
  shoulder, loin or fillet

[broth]

1.6 litres dashi (see page 19)

2 tbsp light soy sauce

2 tbsp soy sauce

2 tbsp sake

1 tsp salt

[to serve]

squeeze of yuzu juice

shichimi pepper or *sansho*
  powder, to taste

See photograph on page 199

1. Peel the daikon, make incisions along the length of the daikon at 1.5cm intervals, then shave the daikon using a peeler to make noodle-like strips.

2. Wash the watercress and drain well. Trim the woody stem ends.

3. Combine the ingredients for the broth in a saucepan and place over a medium heat. When it comes to the boil, add the daikon, let it cook for a few minutes, then add the pork. Finally, add the watercress just before turning off the heat. Pour into serving bowls, squeeze over some yuzu and garnish with *shichimi* pepper or *sansho* powder, to taste.

豚汁

Pork and vegetable miso soup

[Serves 4]

5 cm piece of daikon (200 g)

5 cm piece of carrot (100 g)

½ burdock root or 1 parsnip (100 g)

1 piece konnyaku (200 g), optional

2–3 small potatoes or Japanese taroes (180 g)

200 g thinly sliced pork ribs

1.2 litres dashi (see page 19)

5–6 tbsp miso (see page 78)

[to serve]

baby leek or Japanese leek or spring onion, chopped and soaked in water

shichimi pepper

See photograph on page 202

1. Peel the daikon and carrot, cut them in quarters lengthways, and slice them into 5 mm quarter-rounds (*icho-giri*, see pages 228–230).

2. Peel the burdock root and shave into slices (*sasagaki-giri*, see pages 232–4). Alternatively, peel the parsnip and cut it into thin shavings.

3. If using, tear the konnyaku into pieces and boil it in water to remove the bitterness, then drain.

4. Peel the potatoes or taroes and cut horizontally into rounds or half-moons (*hangetsu-giri*, see pages 228–230). Soak in water, then drain.

5. Cut the pork into bite-sized pieces.

6. Heat the dashi in a saucepan and add the daikon, carrot, parsnip, konnyaku (if using) and potatoes. Skim the surface when the broth comes to a boil and lower the heat.

7. When the vegetables are soft, add the pork and simmer until the pork is cooked through, then dissolve the miso into the broth.

8. Pour into a serving bowl and serve with the chopped spring onion and *shichimi* pepper, scattered over to taste.

豚汁
Pork and vegetable miso soup

This is a favourite dish of the Japanese. You can learn various ways to cut vegetables in making this recipe, so I often choose this dish when teaching cooking techniques to children.

ゆず I Yuzu

Root vegetables such as lotus root, green vegetables such as mizuna and citrus fruits including yuzu – I have so many favourite Japanese ingredients and many of them are essential to my recipes.

Among them, yuzu is the flavour whose season I look forward to the most. When yuzu is in season, I squeeze it directly on to meat, fish and vegetables as you would a lemon. Even the tiniest amount of yuzu zest can enhance the original taste of the dish but, when it's in season I enjoy the luxury of using plenty of shredded yuzu zest. Yuzu soy sauce, a mixture of yuzu juice and soy sauce, is an important seasoning in my house; we use it in all sorts of ways – as a dipping sauce for hot-pots to vegetable dressings and stir-fried food. During its season, I make enough yuzu soy sauce for one year and store it in the refrigerator or freezer.

As Japanese food has become more popular internationally, it has become easier to find Japanese ingredients overseas. However, such seasonal ingredients such as yuzu remain difficult to obtain. When I introduce recipes to people living outside Japan, I usually substitute unusual ingredients with those that they can easily obtain because I hope as many people as possible will try and enjoy my style of cooking without any difficulties. At the same time, I hope that more and more people realise how delicious these Japanese seasonal ingredients are. If you have the opportunity, do buy them and experience these seasonal ingredients for yourself.

ゆず

Yuzu

Yuzu is a kind of citrus fruit. There are two types of yuzu: yellow yuzu is harvested from autumn to winter when the fruit is ripe; green yuzu is harvested before the fruit is ripe, from early summer to early autumn. Yuzu has a unique fresh aroma. The flesh is so sour that it is not eaten, but the juice is used as a seasoning to add aroma and tartness to dishes. Thinly shaved slices of the zest are also used for flavour. As the white part beneath the zest is very bitter, only the surface of the zest is shaved and used. This fruit is not only used in cooking – people also put yuzu in their bath and enjoy its fragrance in wintertime.

4

甘味

DESSERTS

スパイスシフォンケーキ
Chiffon cake

I usually start my working day by enjoying a cup of tea and some sweet treats with my colleagues. I started out as a staff member working behind the scenes for a TV cooking show. But even back then, I told myself that I would cherish morning teatimes if I ever became a cookery writer. It was this chiffon cake that I practised over and over in anticipation of that day. Even now, when I make this cake, it reminds me of those days and I feel proud to have come this far. At the same time, it makes me more determined to do even better.

スパイスシフォンケーキ
Chiffon cake

[makes 1 x 24cm cake]

180g granulated sugar

10 large eggs, separated

100ml vegetable oil

100ml water

220g flour

1 tbsp baking powder

[spices]

½–1 tbsp ground
   cinnamon

1 tsp ground allspice

1 tsp ground cloves

2 tbsp caraway seeds

icing sugar, to dust

*See photograph on page
   208*

1. Preheat the oven to 160°C, Gas Mark 3.
2. Add half the granulated sugar to the egg yolks and beat well with a whisk until thick.
3. Add the vegetable oil and the water and mix well.
4. Sift in the flour and baking powder and mix lightly with a whisk. Add the spices and mix until all the flour is incorporated and the batter is smooth.
5. Make the meringue: in a separate bowl, beat the egg whites with an electric whisk until soft peaks form. Add the remaining granulated sugar and beat until it forms stiff peaks.
6. Add a third of the meringue to the cake batter and fold in with a rubber spatula. Repeat this process with the rest of the meringue and fold in quickly but gently until the mixture is an even colour.
7. Pour the mixture into a 24cm ring cake tin from a height. Gently lift and drop the pan several times on your work surface to get rid of any air bubbles from the batter.
8. Bake for 45–55 minutes. Take the tin out of the oven, turn it over on to a cooling rack and leave to cool completely upside down in the tin.
9. When cool, flip over again, carefully run a knife around the edges, taking care not to scratch the pan and carefully turn out onto a serving plate.
10. Cut the cake into slices and arrange on a plate. Dust with icing sugar before serving.

小倉アイスクリーム
Ogura ice cream

This is a Japanese-style dessert made by adding shop-bought boiled adzuki beans to vanilla ice cream. Once you learn how to make the basic vanilla ice cream, you can make your own flavour variations by adding fruit, such as strawberries, blueberries and raspberries, instead of adzuki beans.

小倉アイスクリーム

Ogura ice cream

[Makes about 600ml]

2 eggs

50g granulated sugar

200ml double cream

100g shop-bought sweet adzuki bean paste (with skins)

200g shop-bought cooked adzuki beans

See photograph on page 213

1. Beat the eggs in a bowl, add half the sugar and mix well using a whisk.

2. Pour the double cream into a separate bowl, add the remaining granulated sugar and whisk until you have stiff peaks.

3. Pour the egg and sugar mixture into the cream mixture and stir to combine. Pour this mixture into a shallow container, cover with clingfilm and put in the freezer.

4. After about 30 minutes, as it starts to freeze, take it out of the freezer and mix in the adzuki bean paste and the beans, then return to the freezer. Stir the mixture at regular 30-minute intervals while it freezes to break up the ice crystals. Once frozen, serve.

パンナコッタ

Panna cotta

[Makes 8–10]

5 g powdered gelatine

2 tbsp water

300 ml milk

½ vanilla pod

60 g granulated sugar

200 ml double cream

2 tbsp rum

[caramel sauce]

50 g granulated sugar

1 tsp water

50 ml hot water

See photograph on page 216

1. Sprinkle the powdered gelatine evenly over the 2 tablespoons water in a small bowl and set aside.
2. Pour the milk into a saucepan. Split the vanilla pod lengthways and scrape out the seeds. Add the pod and the seeds to the milk and place over a low heat. Add the granulated sugar and stir until dissolved.
3. Turn the heat off just before it comes to the boil. Remove the vanilla pod and add all of the diluted gelatine. Stir and let it dissolve.
4. Add the double cream a little at a time while mixing, then add the rum for a spritz of flavour.
5. Prepare a bowl of iced water and cool the saucepan in it, whisking the contents all the time until it cools and thickens slightly.
6. Pour the mixture into small serving bowls and chill in the refrigerator until set.
7. Make the caramel sauce: Put the granulated sugar and the 1 tsp water into a small saucepan and heat gently. When the colour starts to change, shake the pan and cook over a low heat until it turns light amber. Remove from the heat and add the hot water. When it cools, pour the sauce over the panna cotta.

パンナコッタ
Panna cotta

―――――――――

 I have been making this dessert for a long time and it is one of my family's favourites. The rum gives it an adult flavour. I also use a small amount of gelatine to give it a creamy texture that melts in your mouth. This is a dessert that everyone loves.

失敗しないチーズケーキ
Foolproof cheesecake

People often think that baking cakes and desserts is difficult. But with this cheesecake, all you have to do is to mix the ingredients in one bowl and then bake. The result will be delicious, even if you are baking it for the first time. I often make this to give as a gift, decorating it with a tiny bouquet of herbs from my garden.

失 敗 し な い チ ー ズ ケ ー キ
Foolproof cheesecake

[makes 1 x 18cm round cake]

100g digestive biscuits

30g butter (salted or unsalted), at room temperature

200g cream cheese, at room temperature

90g granulated sugar

2 eggs

200ml double cream

3 tbsp flour

1 tbsp lemon juice

icing sugar, to dust

See photograph on page 219

1. Preheat the oven to 160–170°C, Gas Mark 3–3½. Line the base and sides of an 18cm diameter springform cake tin with baking paper.

2. Put the biscuits into a plastic food bag and coarsely crush them with a rolling pin, then mix in the softened butter. Tip the contents of the bag into the tin and press the crumbs evenly and firmly into the base.

3. In a bowl, beat the cream cheese with a hand-held electric whisk until soft and smooth.

4. Add the sugar and then eggs and mix well. Add the double cream and mix well until the mixture thickens.

5. Sift in the flour and fold in lightly with a rubber spatula. Add the lemon juice and mix again.

6. Pour the batter into the tin. Gently lift and drop the tin several times on your work surface to get rid of any air bubbles. Bake for 40–45 minutes.

7. Remove from the oven and set aside to cool in the tin. Once the cheesecake has cooled, remove from the tin and chill in the refrigerator.

   * Baked cheesecake can be stored in the freezer.

8. Cut into slices and dust with icing sugar to serve.

ふわふわパンケーキ

Fluffy pancakes

[Makes four 12cm pancakes]

100ml natural yogurt (unsweetened)

30g granulated sugar

2 eggs, separated

50ml milk

100g flour

1 tsp baking powder

vegetable oil or butter, for frying

butter, jam, maple syrup, for toppings

See photograph on page 222

1. Place a colander over a bowl and line the colander with kitchen paper. Put the yogurt in and cover with clingfilm. Let it stand for at least 1 hour in the refrigerator to drain the excess liquid from the yogurt.

2. Add a third of the sugar to the egg yolks in a bowl and mix well with a whisk. Add the drained yogurt and milk and mix well.

3. Add the remaining sugar to the egg whites and whisk with an electric whisk until you have stiff peaks.

4. Sift the flour and baking powder into the sugar, egg and yogurt mixture and fold in with a rubber spatula.

5. Add a third of the whisked egg whites to the flour and yogurt mixture and mix in. Add the remaining egg whites and fold in gently so as not to knock out too much of the air.

6. Heat some vegetable oil or butter in a frying pan over a medium heat. Pour in a quarter of the batter. Reduce the heat and cover with a lid. When the edges are cooked, flip it over and cook through. Repeat this process with the remaining batter to make 4 pancakes.

7. Serve fresh out of the pan with your choice of toppings, such as butter, jam or maple syrup.

ふわふわパンケーキ
Fluffy pancakes

These pancakes are especially fluffy because of the addition of airy egg whites. Whisking up the egg whites requires a bit of effort, but it's definitely worth it. When I taught this recipe at the college in Hawaii, everybody told me they had never tasted pancakes this good. I was so happy to hear that.

母ドーナツ
Mom's doughnuts

My mother taught me how to make these doughnuts a long time ago and this recipe brings back happy memories. My mother didn't make many sweet things, but she often made these doughnuts because they were my father's favourite. A very loose dough is the secret to making these doughnuts.

母 ド ー ナ ツ

Mom's doughnuts

[Makes 10 ring doughnuts and 10 doughnut holes]

2 eggs

80g caster sugar, plus extra
for sprinkling

50ml milk

40g melted butter

250g bread flour, plus extra
for dusting

2 tsp baking powder

vegetable oil, for deep-frying

ground cinnamon,
for sprinkling

See photograph on page 224

1. Crack the eggs into a large mixing bowl and whisk. Add the sugar and mix well.

2. Add the milk and melted butter and continue to mix well.

3. Sift the flour and baking powder into the mixture and mix well with a rubber spatula until smooth.

4. Tip the dough out on to a floured piece of parchment paper. Roll it out to a thickness of 1.5cm. Dust more flour over the top and loosely cover with clingfilm. Let it rest in the refrigerator for at least 3 hours until the dough firms up.

5. Remove the dough from the refrigerator. Use a floured doughnut cutter to cut doughnut shapes – flour the cutter each time. The dough will be very soft, so handle it carefully.

6. Heat the oil to 180°C in a large saucepan and deep-fry the doughnuts, a few at a time, turning regularly to avoid burning, for 2–2½ minutes until they are golden brown and cooked through. Take out the smaller doughnut holes first as they will cook more quickly.

7. For plain doughnuts, sprinkle with plenty of sugar and toss to ensure they are coated all over while still hot. For cinnamon doughnuts, sprinkle first with sugar, then with a light dusting of ground cinnamon.

野菜の切り方
How to cut vegetables

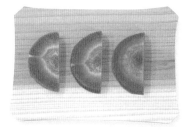

半月切り

Hangetsu-giri
(half-moons)

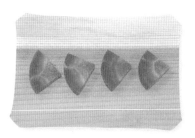

いちょう切り

Icho-giri
(quarter-rounds)

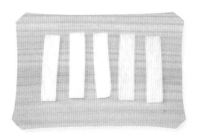

短冊切り

Tanzaku-giri
(rectangles)

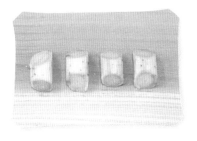

乱 切 り

Ran-giri
(random shapes)

く し 形 切 り

Kushigata-giri
(wedges)

野菜の切り方
How to cut vegetables

半 月 切 り
Hangetsu-giri (half-moons)

Used for cutting cylindrical vegetables such as carrots, daikon radish and turnips into half-moons. Cut the vegetables in half lengthways, then slice crossways to your desired thickness.

い ち ょ う 切 り
Icho-giri (quarter-rounds)

Used for cutting cylindrical vegetables such as carrots, daikon radish and turnips into quarter-rounds to resemble a ginko leaf. Cut the vegetables in half lengthways, then in half again, then slice crossways.

短 冊 切 り
Tanzaku-giri (rectangles)

Cut the ingredients into pieces of the desired length and width, then slice them finely into thinner pieces. Suitable for cutting nori or vegetables for stir-fried dishes and soups.

乱切り

Ran-giri (random shapes)

Used for cutting ingredients into random but even-sized pieces. Cut the ingredient diagonally against the grain then rotate it. This ensures a large surface area of the ingredient, so you can cook these random-shaped wedges quickly and season them thoroughly. Suitable for cutting ingredients for simmered dishes and soups.

くし形切り

Kushigata-giri (wedges)

Used to cut spherical ingredients such as onions, tomatoes and lemons into wedges. Cut the ingredient in half, then into even-sized wedges.

野菜の切り方
How to cut vegetables

そぎ切り

Sogi-giri
(shaving cut)

ささがき

Sasagaki-giri
(*sasagaki* shavings)

長ねぎの
みじん切り

Fine chopping
(for Japanese leeks)

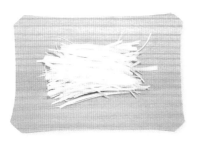

白髪ねぎ

Shiraga-negi
(matchsticks)

野菜の切り方

How to cut vegetables

そ ぎ 切 り

Sogi-giri (shaving cut)

Used for shaving ingredients very thinly. Place a knife with the blade flat against the ingredient and shave it by carefully pulling the knife towards you. Suitable for ensuring the even thickness of pieces or to shave ingredients with a large surface area.

さ さ が き

Sasagaki-giri (*sasagaki* shavings)

Sasagaki is one way to slice vegetables and is used for shaving long, narrow vegetables such as Japanese burdock root. Keep the vegetable in your hand and while you rotate it, shave or slice thinly downwards with a knife as if sharpening a pencil.

長ねぎの
みじん切り

Fine chopping
(for Japanese leeks)

Make scores in an ingredient with the tip
of a knife, then slice it widthways into
small pieces. If necessary, chop these
into smaller pieces.

白髪ねぎ

Shiraga-negi
(matchsticks)

Used for thinly slicing ingredients such
as spring onions into matchsticks. Cut
the ingredient into 4 cm lengths. Score
the pieces lengthways, open them and
if necessary remove any core. Unfold
and pile the remaining layers of the
ingredient and cut along the grain into
matchsticks. Soak them in water, drain
and use as a garnish for noodles and
other dishes.

INDEX

An Hachette UK Company
www.hachette.co.uk

First published in Great Britain in 2020 by Conran Octopus,
an imprint of
Octopus Publishing Group Ltd
Carmelite House
50 Victoria Embankment
London EC4Y 0DZ
www.octopusbooks.co.uk

By arrangement with NHK Publishing, Inc., Tokyo,
in care of Tuttle-Mori Agency, Inc., Tokyo
Original Japanese edition published in 2018 by NHK Publishing, Inc.

ISBN 978 1 84091 808 3

A CIP catalogue record for this book is available from
the British Library.

Printed and bound in China

1 3 5 7 9 10 8 6 4 2